THE UNITY CODE

THE UNITY CODE

Rewriting the Twin Flame Template
for Your Sacred Union Path of Ascension

SUSAN DAWN

PENNSYLVANIA

This book contains concepts, advice, and information relating to spirituality, individual welfare, and interpersonal well-being. It is not intended, nor shall it be treated, as a substitute for professional advice or services. The views and opinions expressed in this book are the author's own. While all efforts have been made to ensure the accuracy of the information contained in this book as of the date of publication, any use of such information is at the reader's sole discretion and risk. Neither the author nor the publisher shall be held liable or responsible for any loss, claim, or damage allegedly arising out of the use, or misuse, of the information or suggestions in this book.

This book contains the poem, "Poem for the Divine Feminine," written by Susan Dawn as part of Susan Dawn Spiritual Connections (2022).

Susan Dawn Spiritual Connections, LLC
Lititz, PA
www.susandawnspiritual.com

Library of Congress Control Number: 2024908392
ISBN Hardback: 979-8-9882881-3-8
ISBN Paperback: 978-1-7379707-7-4
ISBN Ebook: 978-1-7379707-8-1

Cover Design by Andrew Brown, designforwriters.com
Interior Design by Rebecca Brown, designforwriters.com

Visit the author's website at www.susandawnspiritual.com

Printed in the United States of America

"When love has fused and mingled two beings in a sacred and angelic unity, the secret of life has been discovered so far as they are concerned; they are no longer anything more than the two boundaries of the same destiny; they are no longer anything but the two wings of the same spirit."

Victor Hugo, *Les Miserables*

CONTENTS

A NOTE FROM
SUSAN DAWN

I SUPPOSE I'LL START AT the beginning, but the truth is, I don't exactly know where that is. Is the beginning when I was unexpectedly activated to my ascension by a Twin Flame connection, launching me on a journey home to myself? Is the beginning fifteen years ago when I experienced my first major spiritual awakening in the sacred mountains of France? Is the beginning another decade or two before that when I first met my counterpart, though I wouldn't recognize him as anything other than a classmate at the time, or further back to *the* beginning.

Yes, *that beginning.*

Maybe I'll start with my story, and we'll see how it unfolds. After all, isn't that the heart of this journey itself?

My deep desire to understand myself began in the pages of my earliest diary and would translate to a personal blog years later, where I would then spend over a decade attempting to figure out who I am and why I'm here and why the world is the way it is (and how to change it for the better). That journey of discovery didn't seem to have a place in Sunday services, where I was encouraged to follow others' truths rather than explore my own. I felt disconnected from myself and from God, more confused by faith than calmed by it. I always sensed there was something more, something that religion itself couldn't provide. It seemed we were part of an infinite puzzle, its pieces scattered throughout the Universe, and religion held only one piece of it. I wanted the rest of the puzzle. I wanted the big picture. I wanted to know more.

Something was waking up inside me even at that young age—a spark of truth igniting in my soul, though I didn't have a name for it. I wanted a name for it. I wanted to know myself, to figure out where I belonged. And so, I began to research other faiths, hoping one of them would speak to me, that I would have that "a-ha!" moment and the rest of the pieces would fall into place. The problem was that all of them spoke to me.

Instead of belonging somewhere, I felt like I belonged everywhere.

The more I explored, the more I realized my beliefs weren't founded in religion. At least, not in any one religion, and certainly not one I could name. The fundamentals of what I believed, however—what felt true beyond my cognitive understanding— crossed those boundaries. Life stems from a source, and that source is Love.

When I was in my early years of high school, I read a quote from Thomas Paine's *Rights of Man* in which he wrote, in summary, "My country is the world and my religion is to do good." Those words resonated with me like nothing else.

Simple. Honest. Maybe it really wasn't as complicated as we made it seem.

It made more sense than anything else I'd read or studied. Religion was too confining for me, too structured. There were too many unanswered questions, and I couldn't accept that faith meant being led blindly when we have the capability of seeing for ourselves.

Faith, I began to understand, was about trusting your truth.

So, I began the journey of discovering what my truth was…

Catalyst events of multiple losses, chronic illness, and meeting soul connections plunged me deeper than ever into the core of myself and my connection with God. Of course, I went kicking and screaming. My human self, so scarred by past experiences, didn't know how to let go and surrender, and though spirituality seemed so easy and simple when I was younger, I'd since lost my faith and lost myself. I felt fragmented, betrayed and abandoned by the Universe that I had once been so connected to. My anger at God for this suffering created a separation within myself. Why would a benevolent God desert us in our time of greatest need? How could faith be asked of us when there was so much pain in the world? What was faith, anyway?

Slowly, as I began to heal my health, I also began to heal my spirit. I started to understand that these experiences weren't for the purpose of pain but love. Strength. Courage. God was giving me everything I would need to walk through the illusion of who I thought I was in order to come home to myself.

In 2017, when I was activated to the next level of my spiritual journey through meeting my Twin Flame, a former childhood classmate, I was initiated into a process of ultimate surrender— opening my mind, expanding my heart, and placing my full trust in the Universe to guide me on my soul's path. The more I opened up to parts of myself I had forgotten or suppressed, the more at home I felt.

I was connecting to God again.

I began my YouTube channel, *Susan Dawn Spiritual Connections*, a year later after hearing the call from the Universe. Of course, I resisted at first. I didn't know what I was doing or why I was being guided in this new direction—and have I mentioned yet how stubborn I can be? But I knew from past experiences what it meant to trust the soul-nudge, and over the months that followed, I explored where I was being led as I deepened my connection to myself and to God. My YouTube channel became the story of my own spiritual evolution as much as it grew into a community of support and empowerment for others along their personal paths.

Through those channelings and my personal counterpart connection, an understanding of sacred partnerships and Twin Flames expanded from a relationship template to an evolution of the soul. My ascension journey was formed on the foundation of these principles, tools, and understandings, which have since become their own template for conscious connections within the realm of unity consciousness.

This book is a compilation of years of sacred channelings and first-hand experiences around what I call Ascension Relationships—specifically those known as Twin Flames, Sacred Partners, and Higher-Level Soulmates.

My definitions of the varying types of soul connections, including Karmic Connections, Soulmates, and Twin Flames, may differ from yours. This book is meant to be only a piece of your puzzle as you follow the path of your heart to discover your inner truth.

Here are a couple of key points that serve as the foundation for my beliefs guiding this book:

∞ It's been my experience working with hundreds of clients and the collective community that spiritual connections are meant to launch individuals on their soul growth journey into self-love and spiritual ascension. This journey is not about being beholden to labels or connections themselves but about learning to trust yourself and your inner guidance. No psychic, reader, guru, or guide can ever replace your own knowing about your personal experiences or connections. (Nope, not even me!)

∞ While the labels are useful in translating energy, communicating feelings and intentions, and differentiating between the soul connections (something that must be felt to be understood), the terms themselves can be too restrictive to what is truly something spiritual—the depth for which there is often a lack of words available. Again, please trust your journey and follow your soul's resonance. You and only you can know for yourself what type of spiritual connection you're experiencing.

∞ The physical relationship with a Twin Flame or sacred partner is very much part of the connection, just as it's part of any connection. However, we can often get caught up in the physical relationship and lose sight of our spiritual purpose. In this book, we'll be focusing primarily on the energetic connection between counterparts.

∞ A conscious relationship is a reflection of love. While counterparts may trigger each other to bring up wounds and projections within their unconscious state, the Twin Flame or sacred partner label is not meant for you to attach to, justify, excuse, or tolerate disrespectful, toxic, or abusive behavior in any way.

∞ The emphasis of this journey is on our individual soul growth to self-empower and strengthen one's sovereignty and self-love, even through partnership with another. Many of these teachings focus on self-accountability, as each partner is responsible for their own healing.

∞ Finally, I wish to express that my personal experience on this ascension journey is the lens through which I was guided to create my platform and spiritual practice nearly a decade ago. I don't have, nor have I ever had, any affiliation with Twin Flame-specific communities or other spiritual groups. This book is an extension of my platform and practice and is meant for those experiencing spiritual connections who want to understand themselves and their relationships with others, GodSource, and the world from a higher perspective of soul growth and self-love while also enjoying the human experience.

We all play a part in one another's expansion, and as I've continued in my spiritual evolution as part of the collective, my beliefs have developed as well. I respect everyone's personal journey, and I appreciate being able to share my truth and story as part of this ever-evolving experience.

ABOUT THIS BOOK

At *Susan Dawn Spiritual Connections*, we look at spiritual topics and teach or channel through a wider energetic lens. These teachings and channelings are expressed from a holistic spiritual perspective without adherence to the dogma or doctrine of one specific religion or fundamental belief. We believe spirituality is an internal journey in which there are countless paths of personal evolution.

My beliefs were formed within a foundation of Christianity; however, I also have personal connections to and have studied Judaism, Buddhism, Hinduism, and other world religions. It's through this holistic lens that we share our teachings and channelings for this ascension journey. We welcome all who approach with an open mind and heart as we, too, continue to grow and evolve. Please use your discernment and trust your intuition for what resonates for you.

The Unity Code is a nondenominational book focused on the journey of personal spiritual growth as experienced through sacred relationship with another.

What this book is not:

+ This book is not a blueprint for how to get into union.
+ This book is not a template for physical relationship with your Twin Flame or sacred partner.
+ This book is not a doctrine but rather an approach to understand and explore your soul's journey.

In this book, we use the term Twin Flame/Sacred Partners interchangeably with the preferred label of Divine Counterparts, or counterparts. I want to emphasize that the labels for these connections are, at the end of the day, inconsequential. At the energetic soul level, it's all just love, which is what we're coming home to and remembering. But we're also human, and having these human experiences—particularly as part of our spiritual awakening or ascension journey—can be confusing as we navigate our way to this higher understanding. That's what *The Unity Code* is about—it's not to box you in but to help liberate you from what you think you know to become more of all that you really are.

The teachings in this book will especially resonate for those who consider themselves Divine Feminine energy or who are on what's known as a Twin Flame Journey, as this is the perspective that's personally shared. However, you can also apply these teachings to all conscious connections to help you experience healthier relationships. This book was written to guide you to a higher-level understanding of soul connections, sacred union, and ascension as a path for embracing unity consciousness and oneness with yourself and others.

Union is already part of you, and so is your Twin Flame.

This is the hallmark of *The Unity Code*.

INTRODUCTION

SACRED PARTNERS, ALSO CALLED TWIN Flames/Twin Souls or Soulmates, are conscious relationships propelling us on our spiritual path towards healing, self-love, and unity consciousness. While soulmates are our perfect matches in terms of compatibility in which the relationship develops with relative ease and familiarity, Twin Flames are of a higher frequency and act as our perfect mirrors, reflecting the sacred within the shadow while helping us remember what it means to experience and embody true, unconditional love on a journey of soul growth and expansion.

Counterparts possess complementary traits—in essence, the very definition of yin and yang—to come into perfect wholeness within the self and in sacred relationship with one another. They embody the masculine and feminine energies and share the exact same frequency or "soul song," which is why, when they meet, it's a shockwave of instant attraction, familiarity, and, indeed, love.

Generally, we don't know what it means to be loved… At least, not deeply, truly, and unconditionally loved because that's a rare thing in a world of expectations and limitations. So, when someone comes along, sharing their heart and showing you your own, it seems like a foreign language only your soul knows and that you desperately want to understand.

Sacred partnerships can be challenging because counterparts serve the purpose of catalyzing each other's journey, helping each other to heal, grow, and expand through more profound levels of spiritual awakening. Through this growth, they collectively shift the planet to a new template of connection, relationship, and, ultimately, love. This mission is, at its core, a shift into unity consciousness. When two counterparts come into genuine harmony of their masculine and feminine energies within themselves and in their physical connection, their mission is accelerated, with divine love rippling outward towards all of life, making these connections truly sacred.

As part of this ascension process, counterparts often trigger each other to release lifetimes' worth of karma and subconscious fears and blocks. This triggering, while it can feel deeply painful, isn't without purpose either. The resulting transformation raises the energetic frequencies and helps the soul ascend to a higher state of love, replacing separation consciousness with unity consciousness as we remember our divinity.

MY STORY

I haven't held back from sharing my personal ascension process because I believe being open about our experiences reminds us we're not alone and helps us better navigate the road ahead. Even before I was consciously undergoing a spiritual awakening and ascension, I was posting about my self-development, my writing and publishing process, and then my diagnosis and recovery from Lyme disease. All of these experiences are part of my life story, and my ascension journey is simply another aspect of that evolution.

Well, maybe not so simply. I always say ascension is a whole other ball game…

I've been a spiritual person my whole life, though I didn't always consider myself one. I have memories of sitting on the pink carpet of my childhood bedroom, talking to angels and connecting with Mother Mary. I attended my childhood best friend's Jewish holidays and enjoyed reading *Siddhartha* and *Jonathan Livingston Seagull* in school without knowing they were spiritualist books. In fact, as a voracious reader, most of my early studies came from books, including my natural gravitation towards the Transcendentalists—most notably, Emerson and Thoreau. These books unknowingly set the stage for my spiritual evolution.

My "first" spiritual awakening happened in November 2008 when, at 25 years old, I traveled to a small village near Carcassonne, France to spend a month at an amateur writer's retreat. It was the greatest adventure of my life—and also the most anxiety-ridden. To put it plainly, I was a hot mess. It was my first time solo-traveling to a foreign country, where I would have to navigate planes, trains, and automobiles. On the trip there, everything that could go wrong did. I missed my connecting flight to Toulouse, which inevitably set off a series of missed trains and car rides to the inn where I'd be staying for the month.

This was a time before personal cell phones and social media as we know it today, a time before ride shares and map apps on our phones, a time when lost meant, well…lost. Yet, all along the way, I was guided.

After letting the emotions out with a good cry and calling home every possible moment for moral support, I figured out where I needed to go and sought help to get me there. There was the beautiful woman at the airport ticket counter whose compassionate countenance calmed my nerves as she called the inn. There was the homeless man getting warm in the train station who overheard me sobbing on the phone and cheerfully found me a cab up the mountain ("C'est de mon coeur," he said with a gap-toothed grin, patting his heart while I thanked him profusely). And there was the cab driver himself, Bernard, who sang along to Bruce Springsteen and managed to get a smile out of me as we drove the narrow, winding roads late into the evening. I think I realized then there really are angels among us.

Still, my anxiety was at an all-time high. In the daytime, I helped roll logs down a medieval mountain to be cut for firewood, composted in a cliffside garden, and painted a cold cellar as part of the barter for my room and board. In the evenings, I finished the draft of my first book, *Gold in the Days of Summer*, by a roaring fire in the library and chatted with our small group of fellow writers. It was one such writer who introduced me to Florence Scovel Shinn's 1925 book, *The Game of Life and How to Play It*, though I wouldn't understand energy and manifestation for nearly another decade.

Two weeks into my month-long stay, my nerves still hadn't settled, so the inn owner took me to visit her friend—a psychic medium named Yves who lived in an RV in the middle of the French countryside. It was my first time experiencing Reiki, and afterwards, we sat down for a mediumship session in which my grandmother, who I was extremely close to and who had passed years earlier from Alzheimer's disease, came through. The comfort was palpable, and I'm happy to report that while my return trip of planes and trains wasn't any less stressful with missed connections (again) leading to an overnight stay in the Paris airport, my soul was lighter. I felt stronger and more empowered than I ever thought possible.

Throughout the trip, strangers appeared in seemingly miraculous ways—as if the Universe was showing its support and letting me know I wasn't alone. A middle-aged man temporarily sat near me in the airport café where I and others found resting spots for the night, and we struck up a conversation (in French, no less!) about the old TV series *Columbo*. In Toulouse, a janitor stopped me at the vending machines, reached into one of the shelves of her cleaning cart, and handed me a packaged sandwich she'd bought for her lunch. I paid it forward the next day when the young man in front of me at the café didn't have enough change for his food.

Then there were the dogs every step of the way—even in the airport!—that made me smile and were my sign from God that everything would be okay.

It seems naïve, I know. Even though it wasn't that long ago, it feels like a lifetime, and the world seems so different now. But I love the fact that I was so open back then—love the fact that I could trust the Universe without hesitation. While I like to think I've grown much more practical and necessarily cautious, I've seen evidence of that same magic flowing through my life and the lives of those around me. It's indicative of how it could be, how it should be. People helping people.

I'll always believe in that.

Fifteen years later, in September 2023, I visited England and France on a spiritual pilgrimage for my 40th birthday. I stayed with a former client-turned-dear friend and soul sister, and together we manifested perfect weather, joyful interactions, and divinely guided, memorable experiences. We traveled to Carcassonne, France in a full-circle moment that completed a huge phase of my spiritual journey.

Still, there was so much more of my story in between. My first trip to France had been the catalyst for that first spiritual awakening, launching me into a Dark Night of the Soul and an intensive self-exploration. Returning home, I began a deeper dive into personal development and inner growth. It was around this time that I connected with a local psychic medium who would become a spiritual mentor and personal friend, and I began to take psychic development courses and read spiritual books with intention.

In the middle of this, I continued to experience health issues that had plagued me for most of my life, including an unrelenting fatigue that haunted me throughout my childhood and into young adulthood. Despite these health issues, I persevered and created a sense of success for myself, adapting my life to graduate high school and college, then to travel and work in high-stress environments. However, in May 2012, after six months of severe health decline in which I was having neurological and cognitive trouble in addition to serious physical symptoms, I was diagnosed with Lyme disease and other tick-borne diseases, including Babesiosis, Bartonellosis, and Ehrlichiosis. The recovery felt worse than the illness itself, and for a few months, I lost the ability to walk, speak, and function. I was sleeping over eighteen hours a day, dragging myself into work or taking care of my house or my animals for the few hours I was able to stay awake. I was launched into another Dark Night of the Soul, bringing me to my knees in surrender.

During a particularly difficult relapse, I quit my corporate job to focus solely on my healing. It required humility, a release of pride, and a hell of a lot of trust in the Universe. My connection to God had been fractured around this time—I was not only angry at the unfairness of the experience, but I was feeling like a burden to my family and friends and suffering from survivor's guilt, having just lost a friend to cancer. I journaled my way through the pain—stream-of-consciousness writings taking over my notebooks and my blogs where I would, somehow, always find my way back to hope.

Somehow, I always found a reason to stay.

I wasn't able to connect the dots at the time, but this was another spiritual awakening, leading me into the depths of myself.

The whole of 2016 saw even more challenges. My grandmother—my only surviving grandparent—had a stroke, which led to her being moved to an assisted living facility. My family and I spent that summer packing up her house and getting it ready to sell, and as I had practically grown up there as an extension of my own home, I felt a huge chunk of my childhood being stripped away. Through it all, I worked on myself. I began to heal my confidence, began to have faith in God again, and began to love myself and accept where my journey was bringing me.

In the spring of 2017, I mentioned to one of my best friends that I wanted to see the Broadway show *Anastasia* in New York. Somehow, by that September, we had manifested the trip. I took the train into the city—it was my first trip outside of doctors' visits in years, my first trip on my own since France, and my first time wearing denim jeans in months. Considering my wardrobe basically consisted of pajamas and sweatpants for years, this last one was a really big deal!

I felt confident, beautiful, alive. I felt like me again. My best friend was coming in from Chicago, and we rented an apartment somewhere on 56th Street. I'll never forget this apartment. Original, framed artwork covered the walls, an electric keyboard was set up near the entryway, and a selection of trinkets lined the ledge of the picture window overlooking the courtyard—a sea salt lamp, various sculptures, crystals, and an herb bundle.

"I think this guy's my soulmate!" I joked to my best friend.

Little did I know then what was right around the corner…

It was a weekend of magic and miracles. Together, we were manifesting like crazy. We engaged in profound conversations about spirituality and reflected on her own current Dark Night of the Soul. At one point, she mentioned the phrase "Twin Flames" and began to explain a connection she felt with an old boyfriend. While I was knee-deep into my spiritual studies, this was something I'd never heard, and it was like there was a block preventing me from understanding the concept. Even now, years later, I try to remember our conversation, but there's only a blank page in that book.

I wasn't ready then, but I know, in many ways, this was the Universe preparing me for what was to come.

Two months later, on November 22, 2017, I received a message from a childhood classmate. We met for coffee. He walked me to my car. I drove home that night knowing there was something different, something profound, something that I couldn't explain.

Something that was just beginning.

He and I were in the same class in the fourth grade, where he seemed to see something in me that I wasn't yet ready—or willing—to see for myself. Painfully shy, merely ten years old, and foolishly thinking I had a crush on someone else, I didn't return his sentiments. Looking back these many years later, I can see there was more at play here, energetically, but I didn't know it at the time.

Even though we continued in the same school, I don't remember seeing him throughout the rest of our education, though he later shared with me that he would often see me. Inexplicably, I would dream about him over the years—dreams where we would pass in the school hallway or see each other across a crowded field, our eyes locking but no words being spoken. They were dreams I couldn't understand—that I didn't want to understand—and I would try to push them away upon waking.

Life took us on different journeys, and we didn't interact for another decade after graduation. Then, in 2012, we connected again through social media, occasionally commenting on each other's posts. In 2016, we began messaging and sharing memes, bonding through a shared spirituality. At one point, I found myself growing attached to him—maybe even attracted—but even though we were both single, I pulled back. I remember studying his picture, trying to figure out what I was feeling, reminding myself he was a former classmate, and that was it. Anything else was too crazy to consider. We met for coffee at a local diner, and while it was good to see each other, I could feel my body vibrating, like the energy was off. We parted ways with a promise to keep in touch, and every so often, we would send a message catching up.

Until November 22, 2017. It was my grandmother's birthday and Thanksgiving Eve. We met at the same diner. I got there a few minutes before him, turning around right as he was reaching for the door. Our eyes met, and it was the same energy from my dreams—a spark of recognition and familiarity that seemed to go beyond this lifetime but that I didn't consciously understand. We grinned at each other and hugged hello. Throughout our conversation, the energy around us felt palpable—it felt like time stopped, like we were in a cosmic container.

Two months earlier, I'd begun randomly singing the reprise from *The Little Mermaid* in my mind. You know the one: "I don't know when, I don't know how, but I know something's starting right now..." When I got in the car that night to drive home, all I intuitively knew was that, somehow, my life had just been irrevocably changed.

In that one moment, we were activated to the ascension journey—a journey of love and growth and triggers and challenges. A journey of shadow work and healing, of more moments of joy than I ever thought possible and an anchoring of peace within. A journey of connection and authenticity and embodiment. A journey of homecoming.

As spiritual as I thought I'd become throughout my life journey—as self-aware as I was—ascension was something else entirely. It opened up my psychic gifts and moved me to higher levels of potential for my personal life. Over the years, I'd established a publishing imprint for my books and a non-profit to support the Lyme community, but ascension shifted me into even greater purpose and service. With my counterpart as my greatest teacher—leading me deeper into spiritual practice, holding space for me while acting as a catalyst for my triggers, and bringing me back to life in more ways than one—I learned how to protect and clear my energy, to rewrite the programming and beliefs I'd carried with me throughout lifetimes, and to heal from trauma and pain of the past. Most importantly, I mended and deepened my relationship with God.

Meeting my counterpart activated a profound shift in consciousness that has only continued throughout several phases of this journey, bringing me into greater union with myself, my connection, and the world around me. I didn't know this when I turned around at the diner that night, and while I became aware of the Twin Flame Journey fairly quickly—which helped me make sense of the phenomena I was experiencing that was outside the parameters of any connection I'd ever known—it would be several years until I really began to understand and integrate the purpose of this sacred union.

It would be years until I understood The Unity Code.

CHAPTER ONE
ASCENSION CONNECTIONS

"Being loved by someone gives you strength, while loving
someone deeply gives you courage."
– Lao Tzu

RELATIONSHIPS ARE OUR GREATEST CATALYSTS for healing and
expansion, reflecting back to us our connection to ourselves. Intimate relationships, especially, ask us to see and be seen in our
realness, in our raw vulnerability, in our most unguarded moments.
In unconscious relationships, which have been the template of
our society for centuries, we look to our partners to fulfill, gratify,
and validate us, which often leads to control and co-dependency,
among other subtly toxic traits. In conscious relationships, two
self-actualized individuals approach the connection with mutual
support and encouragement for growth, the relationship itself
becoming a nurtured third energy.

Like it or not, we live in a dualistic world of extremes—black and
white, up and down, left and right. Our ascension journey teaches us
the middle path, the wider perspective. Take, for example, temperature. We generally identify temperature as one of two extremes:
something's either hot or cold. But temperature itself isn't only one
or the other—it's an expression of varying degrees of warmth and
coldness. The same can be said for you. You're not just one trait but
multiple aspects of an all-encompassing soul. You might consider

yourself more of a core masculine or core feminine energy, for example (which we'll explore in the next chapter), but it takes both in balance to create the wholeness of all you are. Peering beneath the veil of conscious connections, we see the harmonization of these polarities and how they work together for the strength of a relationship.

When you shift in consciousness, you begin to appreciate there's more to this material world than meets the eye and that everything is energy. As part of this process, you no longer accept what's seen from the human perspective at face value. Instead, you connect with your heart and learn to trust your intuition. The veil thins and lifts, and you distinguish the experiences of the physical world as only a fraction of what's real, available, and accessible.

This world was created from energy and is based in energy. You, yourself, are energy. It stands to reason that the world is so much more than what we've perceived and far more than what we've been programmed to believe—nothing is "just" one thing or another. The book you're holding is made up of billions of microscopic particles revolving at such a speed that they form a tangible object. You, yourself, are comprised of billions of neurons and protons. It's fascinating when you think of it—what it takes for the energy to become tangible. And yet, this is exactly what's happening in every moment and what awakening is about—seeing beyond physical perception. It's about reconciling our spiritual world with physical matter, recognizing we're energetic beings in human form. Our ascension is where we become the bridge between the two.

Ascension isn't just a healing journey but a remembrance—a remembrance of who we are on a soul level, a remembrance of our divinity, a remembrance of our eternal connection to God. Before your awakening, you may have been complacent in the expected routine of attending school, going to work, buying a house, starting a family, raising children, and retiring. We'd become accustomed to this way of living, but now we're moving beyond such a linear perspective. What we once believed isn't all there is. We're understanding there's so much more to our lives, to ourselves, and to the Universe itself. These can all be beautiful, chosen experiences, but life isn't limited to what we've been conditioned to desire or what society requires of us and definitely not what happens to us. As energy, we, too, are creative beings informing our physical experience. We're here to serve as a link between the spiritual and physical, and sacred relationships are at the forefront of the consciousness shift as part of an accelerated journey of this remembrance. Your journey to union is just one of infinite paths of spiritual awakening and ascension—one in which you're exploring your soul's truth through the Twin Flame energy and the embodiment of a divine partnership.

The term Twin Flame has become popular over the past several years, even as its formal roots date back to ancient times and exist within diverse religions under various contexts and labels. In the ancient philosophical text, *The Symposium*, Plato describes man as being one half of one perfect soul, split to create two parts to one whole. In Hinduism, Shiva as the masculine energy and Shakti as the feminine energy merge to form the Shiva-Shakti energy of divine union or oneness. In Christianity, we see this same idea in Adam as the masculine principle and Eve as the feminine. From Mary Magdalene and Jesus to Isis and Osiris to Rhada and Krishna, the concept and energy of Twin Flames are paramount in theology and persist through time.

At a time of global awakening, Twin Flames returning to the collective consciousness is more profound than ever. However, with this recognition comes *a lot* of information that needs to be distilled. What is a Twin Flame connection? How does it differ from other connections? What does it mean for our human experience, and how does it help our spiritual ascension?

We're all connected through the same GodSource energy as unique expressions of the Universe, yet we try to logically analyze our experiences through a more narrowed lens as it relates to our human viewpoint. Thus, we use labels as a way to collectively understand ourselves and our world. This is helpful within the framework of our human experience, but it becomes limiting when recognizing ourselves as spiritual beings. The more we shift in consciousness, the better we're able to hold these two ideas: we can identify with and place labels on these concepts while also recognizing we're not attached to whatever it is we're labeling.

To be able to hold two seemingly opposing ideas is, in fact, an attribute of higher consciousness. It's the middle way in a world of dualistic thinking where there's room for all. For example, we know we're having a human experience, but we're *more* than our human experience. The inverse would be recognizing we're soul while *also* being human. These labels are meant to help us further understand ourselves and our experiences in context with the world around us, not to limit us.

When it comes to soul connections—and every connection is a soul connection on some level—we use the terms "karmic connection," "soulmate connection," and "twin flame/twin soul connection" as a way of identifying within the human experience. Again, these are merely labels used for association and aren't meant to limit or keep us attached to specific people or relationships.

I personally believe every relationship is meant to support us in our soul's evolution. For some connections, this is through recognizing duality, fulfilling energetic contracts, and experiencing contrast. For other connections, this is through heart expansion and helping each other rediscover the divinity within on our journey back to love.

It's also my belief that all connections, no matter the label, have the capacity for strong love and are blessings in our lives for how we grow, learn, and expand if we choose to see beyond the human template and through the wider lens of the soul. Always use your discernment by keeping an open mind and heart and accepting what resonates with your truth. What's shared in this book is only a potential piece of a much bigger puzzle on your personal spiritual journey.

Keeping in mind that these labels are useful in helping us discern the type of connection we're experiencing as a way of navigating our journey, let's look at each soul connection individually.

KARMIC CONNECTIONS

Karmic connections are so named because they help us complete a cycle of karma, or energetic cause and effect. They can be found in the form of family members, friends, acquaintances, co-workers, and even strangers passing on the street. These connections come into our lives for a reason—whether for years or mere moments—with the purpose of helping us learn a distinct lesson, share or support a specific experience, or close out/heal from an energetic cycle. Once the lesson is learned and the karmic cycle is closed, karmic connections may naturally fade away.

Karmic connections can feel like strong soul connections and may even exist in romantic love relationships, but they're here primarily to serve a specific purpose as part of our life journey. These connections tend to receive a negative reputation because they can be difficult experiences, but it's important to never underestimate the value of a karmic connection, particularly when it comes to the soul's growth. From the human perspective, karmic connections can feel challenging and even toxic or abusive, but remember there are still lessons within those experiences that our souls are learning.

I want to pause and be clear that this in no way justifies, negates, or excuses toxic or abusive behavior within a connection, and it's certainly not meant to keep you trapped in a pattern or held in a relationship. Your emotional, mental, and physical safety is of primary importance and should always be prioritized. *Always.* Part of your spiritual journey is honoring yourself so that you recognize you're worthy of healthy, loving relationships, particularly starting with yourself. If you ever have trouble remembering this, simply reach out to our community, and we'll remind you.

Yep, I'm that serious and passionate about this.

Within the context of this book, we're looking at this journey from the soul's perspective, and from the soul's perspective, every connection has value, enabling us the gifts of experience, expansion, and growth especially when it comes to loving ourselves.

Karmic connections are here to support us by helping us learn specific lessons. It is, in essence, karma. Karma is the spiritual principle of Cause and Effect, commonly known as "reap what you sow." While many associate karma with "paying dues," it's simply a neutral energetic response with no positive or negative connotation aside from what our human stories assign it. Karma can be thought of as energy in action—the energy we put into the Universe is the energy that's returned to us.

Let's talk about the Laws of Karma for a minute to get a better understanding of what karmic connections might be teaching us:

The Six Karmic Laws

In Buddhism, there are twelve karmic laws or principles by which it's believed the Universe operates. For the sake of these teachings, we'll look at six of them, all building on each other.

Law of Cause and Effect
Commonly referred to as "reap what you sow," this karmic law is founded on the principle that whatever thoughts, words, and actions (all examples of energy) you put into the Universe, you get back. For example, if you're putting out negative thoughts about

yourself or others, you'll see this reflected in your life as negative experiences. If you're acting generously, you'll experience more abundance or opportunities. It's important to remember that the Universe itself doesn't act on a punishment or reward system—it's simply responding to the emitted energy.

Law of Creation

This law asks you to become an active participant in creating your life not only as a benefit to yourself but as service to the world. The Universe responds to your efforts with opportunities and blessings. It's essentially showing you that you're the creator of your world and, thus, your experiences. This goes hand-in-hand with the Law of Cause and Effect.

Law of Humility

This law states that in order to create change, you must first accept what currently is. This includes taking ownership of the fact that your current reality is a result of your past actions. It's here in this acceptance that you can make new choices and establish a new path.

Law of Growth

This Law of Growth states that our physical world is a reflection of our internal expansion. As we grow and change within, our physical world will grow and change in suit. Simply stated, change doesn't occur from the outside in but from the inside out.

Law of Responsibility

This karmic law states that we must take responsibility for our role in every experience, including how others treat us and how we treat others. The Law of Responsibility releases blame and judgment but asks us to take ownership for our creations. This goes hand-in-hand with the karmic laws above.

Law of Connection

Finally, the Law of Connection states that everything in the Universe is connected. Past experiences create the present, which creates the future. Everything is interconnected, and we're all connected to each other.

When identifying karmic connections, we also have to consider these karmic laws because karmic connections are here to help us grow and expand within our soul's story. A karmic connection can be someone you've known previously in another lifetime with whom there's unresolved energy, or it could simply be another soul that's helping you resolve your karma or evolve within a situation by playing a specific role.

Imagine being on the other side—before incarnating into this human form—and announcing, "Hey, I have this lesson to learn or mission to accomplish. Who wants to help me out?" Another soul then lovingly answers, "Sure, I'll play that role for you." This is the fundamentals of a karmic connection—it's an energetic contract in which experiences are had for soul lessons to be learned, supported, or accomplished, and they can be challenging or beautiful depending on what's needed for the soul's evolution.

We've all been the sinner and the saint, the villain and the hero, the devil and the angel. These roles are played out within the landscape of our human experience for the soul's expansion and may last for a reason, a season, or a lifetime—at least, until the karma's cleared, the experience is complete, and the lessons are learned.

SOULMATES

Soulmates resonate with us on a spiritual or "soul" level and encompass a sense of familiarity, comfort, and home. The

Merriam-Webster Dictionary defines a soulmate as "a close friend or romantic partner with whom one has a unique deep connection based on mutual understanding and acceptance." We'll take this one step further and look at the energetic component of what constitutes a soulmate.

First, let's consider soulmates in the context of our culture. Society defines the soulmate as "The One"—it's someone with whom there's an undeniable connection, a "meeting of the minds," a relationship in which you can be your true, authentic self and where there's absolute compatibility, mutual affection, and innate understanding of each other. We see this concept in literature, music, and film, where the "search for the soulmate" is ingrained in the storytelling.

One of my favorite television sitcoms, *How I Met Your Mother*, is a classic example of this search for "The One," as the series narrates the main character's journey to finding his perfect soulmate. In a brilliantly written sentimental scene, Ted, a romantic through and through, questions his heart when he asks a runaway groom how he knew his bride wasn't the one for him. The groom muses about meeting The One, saying, "It's not something that develops over time. It's something that happens instantaneously. It causes swirling like the water of a river after a storm, filling you and emptying you all at once. You feel it throughout your body, in your hands, in your heart, in your stomach, in your skin. Have you ever felt this way about someone? If you have to think about it, you have not felt it. Everyone does eventually, you just never know when or where."

While society likes to paint a picture of the romantic "One," soulmates can be experienced multiple times in various forms. Soulmates can be family members or "soul family" (non-blood related family), best friends, and romantic partners. They can even be pets, such as in the example of my beloved dog, Riley, who you'll meet in Chapter Four. You might also come across a "kindred spirit"—someone who feels energetically similar to a soulmate but isn't meant to stay in your life for long. In romantic relationships, soulmates can be lifetime partners.

Soulmates are exactly that—*soul mates*. It's a group of souls you've incarnated with for lifetimes, sharing a similar energetic frequency or blueprint and with whom you're extremely compatible. There's a bond of instant connection and familiarity in which you identify and interact with each other. Together, you have a sense of belonging and home, and there's a natural comfort and ease that's felt with one another. Often with soulmates, you'll feel as if you've known each other before. This is because you have! Through other lifetimes as part of your soul group. Soulmates stand the test of time, easily picking up where you left off—which is exactly what you're doing on a soul level with each incarnation.

You'll likely find more and more of these soulmates or members of your soul family coming into your physical experience throughout your ascension. As part of the inner work of your journey, you're clearing the karmic contracts so that those who are meant to support your spiritual evolution will become more soul-oriented than karmic. You'll intuitively recognize these soulmates when you meet them.

To further understand the difference between soulmates and karmic connections, imagine a set of three concentric circles representing energetic rings, each emitting a specific frequency. In this diagram, each soulmate and karmic connection is linked to you as part of your human experience but in various ways and at different energetic vibrations.

You and your Twin Flame are in the center, being the same exact core frequency. Don't worry, we'll get more into Twin Flames in a minute.

In the second ring are your soulmates or soul family. They're closest to you because they resonate most with your vibrational energy. They're the souls that have evolved with you throughout lifetimes with shared values, beliefs, interests, goals, and experiences. They support you on an intrinsic level and reflect love, safety, and community.

The outermost ring depicts karmic connections. These are the outlier connections that help you grow through experiences and lessons but may only be part of your life for specific reasons or seasons. For some, if the lesson isn't being learned, karmic connections can extend for a lifetime; however, they may be fraught with challenges as you operate on different energetic wavelengths.

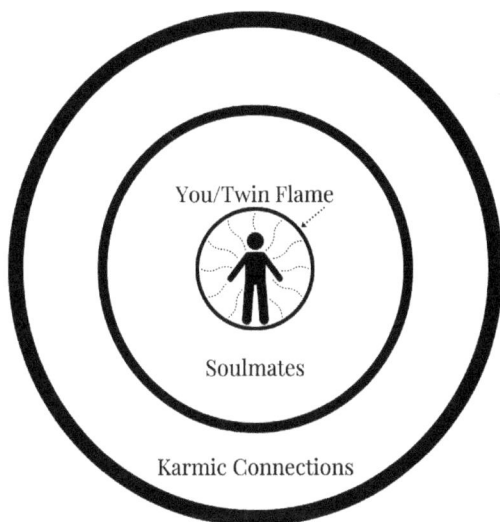

Family members can be soulmates or karmic connections, depending on the role they're meant to play for us and any karmic contracts that are meant to be resolved. Similarly, friends and lovers can be family in what's known as "soul family." Soulmates can help us with karmic lessons, and karmic connections can feel beautiful and loving like soulmates. Each soul has their own soul group or family, and what might be a karmic connection for one individual may be a soulmate to another.

Remember, this is all based on energy versus anything physically identifying. That's why it's so important to emphasize seeing beyond our limited, human perspective of egoic identity. By tuning into your energy, you can begin to understand and discern the difference.

TWIN FLAMES

Twin Flames, also commonly known as Twin Souls or Sacred Partners, are similar to soulmates with the exception that they're one soul experiencing itself in two human embodiments. Unless you've experienced this type of connection first-hand, a Twin Flame dynamic may seem like a fairytale, a delusion, or anywhere in between. Believe me, I've not only heard it all, but I've considered it all for myself! The reason it can be so confusing is due to the depth of such a bond and the soul growth journey that ensues, but this is exactly what distinguishes it from other soul connections.

While soulmates are similar to us in energy, Twin Flames *are* us. The ancient philosopher Plato described this connection as "one soul split into two bodies," yet while most interpret this split soul as missing your other half (which, it can certainly feel this way at times), the one soul is experiencing itself in two physical forms. Twin Flames are the exact same energetic frequency because they are the very same soul.

From a human perspective, you and your Twin Flame will have your individual identities, personalities, and lives. In fact, on the surface, Twin Flames may present as seemingly polar opposites. For example, Twin Flames may show physical differences, have an age gap, be from different religions or cultural backgrounds, or exhibit distinct ways of expressing themselves. However, these differences are only as they appear on the surface, and this, too, is for the purpose of experiencing duality and accelerated expansion.

The soul itself is comprised of Mother-Father Source energy, also known as the feminine and masculine polarity. Twin Flames experience this as divine mirrored polarities of each other. That is, one twin will embody the Divine Feminine energy as their core essence while their counterpart is the embodied Divine Masculine. This may also be seen in healthy conscious connections such as soulmate relationships; however, in Twin Flame connections, the polarities are merged through the process of sacred union wherein the illusion of separation is dissolved and oneness is experienced.

The initial encounter between Twin Flames feels like a shockwave wherein soul recognition is experienced on the deepest level. Remember the description of The One from *How I Met Your Mother*? This also applies to Twin Flames and is why the two connections are often so easily confused; however, Twin Flames chart a different journey. When Twin Flames meet, it feels like you're meeting yourself as you experience a burst of pure love and joy or a sudden serenity—or all of the above! Time seems to stop, and the rest of the world fades away so it's only the two of you in a cosmic embrace. Even the slightest intimacy becomes both a familiar homecoming and an otherworldly experience.

This is the beginning of your ascension, which you may experience as a kundalini awakening. You're seeing each other as you see yourself, including the masks, programming, and patterns of the human self as well as the beauty, compassion, and love of your divinity. While you may have experienced spiritual awakening in the past through other catalyst experiences, this is the start of your soul growth journey.

The term Twin Soul can also be used interchangeably with Twin Flame. While I prefer "sacred partners" or "divine counterparts" to either identifying label, I personally distinguish between Twin Flame and Twin Soul in the following way: Twin Flame reflects the healing process as you return to your authentic truth as soul. It is, in essence, the flame that's ignited between the two. Twin Soul then becomes the next level of the connection, reflecting the harmony between counterparts achieved through the ascension process.

In a channeling many years ago, I was shown the vesica piscis as a metaphor for this sacred union journey. In sacred geometry, the vesica piscis symbolizes the intersection of the spiritual and physical worlds, which may also represent the feminine and masculine polarity in a union of opposites. This is the heart of our ascension.

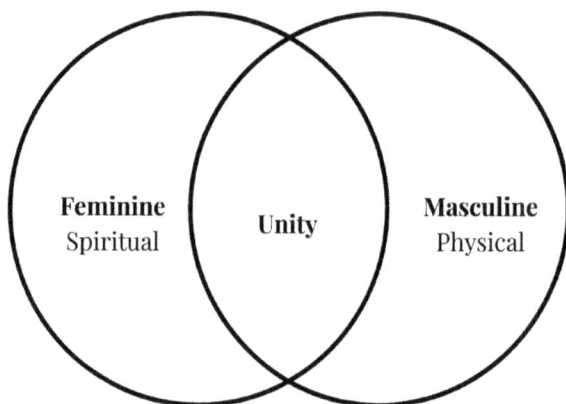

However, to deepen our understanding of the evolution of Twin Flames, I was shown the vesica piscis flipped ninety degrees as a further representation of this process. The first circle illustrates the Twin Flame phase of the journey—the spark of recognition experienced upon meeting and the healing that follows. Next, the intersection represents the soul merge of the Divine Feminine and Divine Masculine, also known as the *hieros gamos* or alchemical marriage.

In this inner union, you balance your masculine and feminine polarities through the process and purification of any remaining dense energies held within lower states of consciousness. This transition then leads to what I like to call the Higher-Heart Ascension. It's here the Twin Flame becomes the Twin Soul to reflect the higher-consciousness state of harmony, joy, and love in the physical union of a sacred relationship.

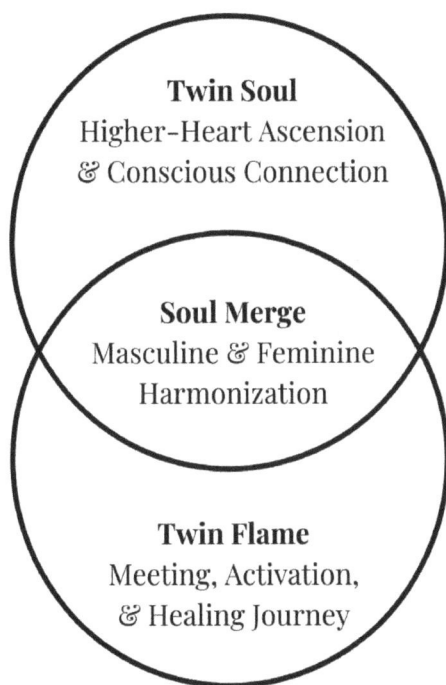

Twin Soul
Higher-Heart Ascension
& Conscious Connection

Soul Merge
Masculine & Feminine
Harmonization

Twin Flame
Meeting, Activation,
& Healing Journey

The Twin Flame and Twin Soul are essentially one and the same. I use these two labels to differentiate between the stages of the journey and the *energies* represented. The Twin Flame might reflect more of the triggers and friction experienced during the healing process, while the Twin Soul reflects the harmony and peace that's embodied as a result of your personal soul growth within conscious connection with your partner.

It's important to remember that these are simply labels to help us understand and navigate our spiritual journey from a human perspective. Because the terms can be so misconstrued within the spiritual community, with degraded connotations placed upon each, I prefer the terms "sacred partners" and "divine counterparts." For the purpose of this book, we'll be using all where appropriate, but as always, I encourage you to tune into your sacred heart to find what resonates most with you.

Clearing Up
the Twin Flame Confusion

Twin Flames are one soul split into two bodies. That is, you're the same soul frequency and energetic blueprint experiencing a second life within this present incarnation on Earth. The reason why the concept of Twin Flames has become so misconstrued is because of the corruption of its spiritual meaning. Many believe that meeting your Twin Flame is simply finding your perfect romantic partner so you can live happily ever after. It's not exactly *wrong*, but this explanation also doesn't paint the full picture, and this human perspective is pretty counterintuitive to what a Twin Flame actually is.

When you meet your Twin Flame, you're meeting yourself.

Your connection with your Twin Flame is a spiritual one and should be honored as such. The easiest way to understand the purpose of such a connection is to think of it as an accelerated ascension. Your soul wanted to evolve and experience everything, and what better way to do so than to live two congruent lives?

One way to picture this is to think of Earth as a school for the soul where you and your Twin Flame are taking different courses for the same college major. For example, one aspect of yourself (your counterpart) is taking a course in American Literature, while another aspect (you, the individual reading this) is taking a course in British Literature. You're both attending the same "university" at the same time, but you're learning from two different vantage points so that when you come together, you can share what you've learned and double the experience for your soul's evolution.

Another example is the scene in *Harry Potter and the Prisoner of Azkaban* where Hermione, ambitious student that she is, doesn't have time for all of the courses she wants to take, so Dumbledore presents her with a time-turner. With this tool, she can essentially duplicate herself by going back in time to take two classes at once. Duplicating, or in the case of Twin Flames, splitting your soul into two human forms, is a way in which you can accelerate your learning and growth. This example also dives deeper into our multidimensional nature and "time is an illusion" teachings that we'll look at later in this book.

Every Twin Flame partnership will experience their journey a little differently. Not all Twin Flames are incarnated on Earth at the same time, and there can be different variations of the Twin Flame energy, such as monadic Twin Flames or Twin Rays. These labels can cause even more confusion to an already baffling experience, so for the sake of this book, we're going to discuss Twin Flames as one soul in two bodies with a sharing of the same higher-self through different life experiences.

While Twin Flames can also present as same-sex partners, for ease of understanding, we'll speak of the masculine or Divine Masculine as male (he/him) and the feminine or Divine Feminine as female (she/her). I want to emphasize, however, that Twin Flame is an *energy* and doesn't adhere to a specific gender. Additionally, while you might embody one or the other as a core energy, you'll generally relate more to the masculine or feminine energy at any given time, as both energies exist within you.

We're getting a little ahead of ourselves, aren't we? Let's backtrack a bit.

Twin Flame as a label helps us differentiate between the various soul connections and what we might be experiencing in our physical-world relationships. However, it's important not to get too caught up in the labels, as this can keep us stuck in what's known as a consciousness trap—a revolving pattern that prevents our evolution. Use the term that feels most comfortable and expansive to you, as what you learn along your sacred union journey can be applied to all connections for healthier, more conscious dynamics.

Over the years, the concept of Twin Flames has become misconstrued due to false teachings and misunderstandings about what Twin Flames really are. While Twin Flame energy is prominently exhibited in our culture, the purpose of such a connection goes beyond the romantic fairytales and Hollywood love stories. This is an old template of relationships based on a very physical-only perspective. It's like looking at a couple holding hands while they walk—you're seeing only the surface layer of romantic expression and not the memories of first meetings, endless conversations, the effort for two people to come together, and the ripple effect their relationship brings to their lives and the lives of those around them. There's always more beneath the surface, a broader story to be told. We live in a very material-driven world, but through our ascension, we begin to understand that everything is energy, everything is connected, and everything is more than what it seems.

In the spiritual community, especially, there's a notable emphasis on the physical relationship with more linear thinking, such as "When will we meet, when will we fall in love, when will we get married, when will we have a family?" These questions, while valid as part of the human experience, are asked because it's the template of third-dimensional consciousness—it's what the ego personality has always known relationships to be. This external focus is also why soulmate connections are often mistaken for Twin Flame relationships.

When you meet or unite with your Twin Flame, there's an eruption of energy—it's an activation of your higher-self and a call for expansion and harmonization within the polarities of the soul. Suddenly, you feel a sense of peace, home, safety, and love deep within the core of your very being. Your meeting goes beyond physical attraction, beyond the logical mind, and while the logical mind will try to pull out all the stops and whistles to make sense of it by boxing it into what it originally knows, the energetic component will override this in a push for surrender to the spiritual nature of the connection. In this initial surrender, your sacred union journey begins.

RECAPPING SOUL CONNECTIONS

Let's take a closer look at the varying types of connections we may experience and why it's important to understand their differences.

First, we have the Twin Flame. To more accurately depict this connection, I should simply list this as "you," as you and your counterpart are energetically one soul. However, you also represent two distinct embodiments within your human identities and unique personalities, and it's the easiest way, for now, to begin to understand this connection. Later in this book, we'll explore higher-level ascension teachings that integrate the concept of the other as you.

Closest to you in frequency are those identified as soulmates. This could be your actual birth family or those who feel like family, your best friends, and your intimate partner. Soulmates include those with whom you're naturally at ease—you might be compatible on a number of different levels and feel like you've known each other for lifetimes, even upon first meeting. This soulmate frequency has a range that can be likened to a radio station. For those closest to you, the sound is crisp and clear, while for others, there might be some static, yet your souls are still tuned to the same station and singing the same song.

Then we have the karmic connections. These connections are here to teach, support, and guide us through our life journeys in specific ways. Karmic connections operate on a frequency that might be furthest from your core energy. In terms of our radio analogy, you might be singing the same song, but you're tuned to different stations. For some connections, it could even feel like one is tuned to an FM radio and another is tuned to an AM radio. These relationships can feel toxic and challenging or loving and guiding, but they're experienced only until the lesson is completed or the soul contract is fulfilled.

For some, karmic connections can include family members, close friends, and significant others who might feel like soulmates, but the energetic resonance differs. That is, the energy that brought you together isn't sustainable because you're operating from different frequencies, and eventually, as you grow, you also grow apart. For others, karmic connections can be co-workers, acquaintances, and even strangers on the street with whom you have brief interactions. These connections are simply here for you to complete a soul contract, resolve karma, support a specific soul mission, or learn from whatever experience you're shown through that particular connection.

Karmic connections are the outliers—those farthest away from your inherent soul frequency—but they provide excellent opportunities for growth and expansion. If we put this on a linear spectrum, for example, it might look like this:

Karmic   **You/**
Connections   **Twin Flame**

Energetic Frequency

←······· **Soulmates**

To simplify this further, let's recap our radio analogy:

+ Karmic Connections: Different radio stations that sometimes play the same song
+ Soulmates: The same radio station playing the same song
+ Twin Flames: You're the song itself

CONSCIOUS CONNECTIONS

Whether we're experiencing a Twin Flame, Soulmate, or Karmic Connection, and whether they're here to uplift and support us or to challenge and catalyze us in our soul growth, we all come from the same Source energy. It's initially helpful to use these labels to identify what each connection is in order to understand our spiritual nature while navigating our human experience, but as we continue to evolve, we realize we can throw out the labels. They don't matter. Ultimately, on a soul level, we're all guiding each other home.

Someone who may be a karmic connection to you may be a soulmate to another, and vice versa. Each connection serves a purpose in the grand design, and when we take a broader look through a spiritual versus physical lens, we see that these connections help us elevate our soul growth journey. The more we can consciously connect with each other in all dynamics, the more we're stepping into unity consciousness.

There are many collective roads to ascension, and each one contains a personal path. The sacred union path of conscious connection is merely one of them. As we shift in consciousness, we begin to recognize there is no separation, that we're connected to all. Every connection is, too, part of the same collective consciousness created from GodSource.

Your ascension journey, whether experienced individually or with a partner, is helping the planetary collective undergo its own process of ascension in which frequencies rise and vibrations shift. This causes a dismantling of unstable structures and is part of the chaos and destruction we're currently seeing in our physical world. The former foundations have to fall away in order for new ways of being to take place, including how we interact and connect with each other. As you heal, expand, and grow on your journey, your energy has a ripple effect on everything around you. It's the cosmic blueprint for why we're here and activated to ascension in this time and space. The individual affects the collective just as the micro affects the macro, and vice versa. Don't forget—everything is interconnected.

Throughout this journey, you're deconstructing all the old templates of connecting, including the past paradigm of relationships and any outdated beliefs that might have served you at one point in your individual experience, but you've since evolved beyond. As you put into practice everything you've learned, utilizing all the tools and resources you've acquired, and begin to embody the sacred self within higher states of consciousness and love, that energetic ripple extends further outwards. Here, you apply your wisdom to healthy, conscious relating so that every encounter becomes a sacred connection.

This is The Unity Code.

CHAPTER TWO
ALL THAT IS SACRED

"Whatever our souls are made of,
his and mine are the same."
– Emily Brontë, *Wuthering Heights*

THE MASCULINE AND FEMININE POLARITY is seen everywhere in our world. Romance languages, for example, use the masculine/feminine to classify nouns: *le soleil* is the French word for sun and classifies as masculine while *la lune* is the French word for moon and classifies as feminine. Interestingly, and perhaps not-so-ironically, the sun is traditionally considered a masculine energy and the moon a feminine energy, which also indicates how masculine and feminine principles present in nature itself.

This masculine and feminine polarity also exists as an archetypal energy within our human embodiment, and while we'll see this most notably in the biologically-represented male or female, we do, in actuality, contain both energies within us. Part of our ascension journey is embracing the energetic union of the two.

But where does this come from? Across ancient times, both the god and goddess-figure were revered; however, in fundamental religions, particularly in modern Christianity, the feminine aspect was stripped to become one Father God in favor of a patriarchal society. Our world as we know it is very fixed and seemingly finite, yet this is a world of illusion—a simulation created from a collective consciousness manifesting in physical form. As we each experience our awakening through our individual healing and internal evolution, we begin to shift the collective consciousness by breaking free from old programs passed down through generations to recognize the power of truth within ourselves.

Our individual ascension journey has a collective ripple effect that advances us out of this past corruption. It's a shift from religion's promise to what's authentic to the soul, for the soul itself holds the blueprint of truth. No longer is there an intermediary in our connection to God. No longer is the feminine energy stripped of her innate place in the world. No longer is she dishonored but recognized in balance with the masculine.

This is GodSource energy—the supreme, pure union of feminine and masculine energy eternally merged as one Mother-Father giving birth to all creation.

In our limited, logical minds it's difficult to fathom oneness. We see the Mother and the Father as separate entities much like our own mothers and fathers. This separation is, at the core, what's being transcended along the ascension journey.

Throughout history, we've been led by a patriarchal system of distorted masculine leadership that's shaped our society and culture, causing feminine energy to be suppressed, persecuted, and oppressed in favor of control, exclusion, and, frankly, full-blown misogyny. Patriarchy has become embedded in politics, economics, and social structures and holds influence over belief systems, values, and even relationships in which the masculine maintains both a physical and moral authority, particularly over the feminine.

Masculine and feminine energies are gender-neutral, but we can notably see patriarchy play out in the physical world in the treatment of females as expressions of the feminine energy. In the United States alone, women weren't allowed to vote until a new amendment was passed by Congress in 1919 as a result of the Women's Suffrage Movement, and it wasn't until 1974 through

the Equal Credit Opportunity Act—a mere fifty years ago!—
that women could legally obtain credit cards in their own name.
This isn't even to mention the subtle ways in which the patriarchy continues to subvert women's rights in the United States
and around the world.

But it's not just women who suffer from a patriarchal system.
Although men undoubtedly benefit from a society that favors them,
according to the American Foundation for Suicide Prevention's
website, there are over one million suicide attempts each year, with
"White males [accounting] for nearly 70-percent of suicide deaths
in 2021." In the following years, that statistic has only increased.
While, of course, factors such as social or economic inequalities
and mental and physical health play a part, it begs the question
of why, in a time when men have every advantage in our society, is
the statistic still so high? It stands to reason that, energetically, at
least, a patriarchal society promoting distorted masculine energy
and precluding divine feminine energy (which we'll discuss shortly)
is damaging to both men and women.

It's important to emphasize here that we're not talking about
the renunciation of masculine energy in favor of femininity as a
war between males and females, and we're in no way suggesting a
shift to a matriarchal society. That would be the other end of the
spectrum, defeating the purpose of balance, wouldn't it? What
we're noting is how the feminine energy, existing in all, has been
suppressed, leading to a toxic and corrupted masculine paradigm
affecting both males and females on a systemic level. Union advo-
cates a holistic approach, similar to what's seen in ancient and
indigenous cultures, as the harmonization of the two.

Imagine, for example, a pendulum similar to the one shown
in the following diagram. This pendulum was affixed to the patriarchy for centuries, creating an energetic imbalance translating
to neglect, rejection, and abandonment of the feminine principle.
Through our collective awakening and ascension—which we can

clearly see in the feminist movement—that previously fixed pendulum is shaken loose, generating energetic momentum that looks like elevated chaos as it moves back and forth before settling into a place of balance. This balance, the union of the two, is what our ascension supports.

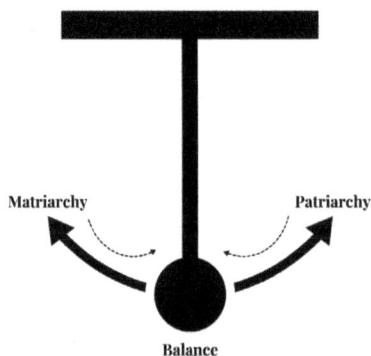

Regardless if you're male or female, or if you consider yourself more of a masculine or feminine embodiment, you energetically contain both the masculine and feminine polarities. One purpose of our collective ascension is remembering the neglected feminine principle within all to bring ourselves and the world into greater harmony.

DEFINING MASCULINE & FEMININE ENERGY

While we all carry both the masculine and feminine archetypal energy within us, and as we're always stepping into one or the other at various points in our daily lives, we also have a core essence—one that feels most natural to us. Each energy holds a distinct template and expresses itself through various traits.

Inner union, or becoming balanced within your inner masculine and feminine energies, is about healing the distortions or unconscious aspects of self and becoming aware of when you're using each. That's not to say you have to constantly analyze yourself. Can you imagine leaving for work and saying, "I have to be in my masculine energy now" or having an expressive conversation with a friend and reminding yourself, "I have to be in my feminine?" Whew! No, thank you! It's simply about being in tune with your own energy and having a conscious awareness of both polarities so that if or when old patterns replay themselves, you can mindfully create a shift. This becomes part of an organic process of embodiment as you let your internal energy guide you.

Let's look at some traits of the masculine and feminine energies:

Masculine Energy	Feminine Energy
Mind	Heart
Active	Patient/Yielding
Doing	Being
Intellect	Intuition
Logic	Vision
Providing	Receiving
Structure	Freedom
Reasoning	Nurturing
Assertive	Introspective
Stable	Supportive
Focused	Creative
Self-Sufficient	Collaborative
Present	Reflective
Grounded	Open/Flowing
Disciplined	Playful
Integrity	Expressive
Rational	Emotional
Firm	Flexible

You might be looking at this list and saying to yourself, "Wait a minute, I resonate with both..." Absolutely, you do! But your core energy will be the one that feels the most natural, without the masks and pressures from the world. If you're a core feminine energy, you'll feel most at home in the creative expression of your emotions and the receptive energy of simply *being*. If you're a core masculine energy, you'll feel most comfortable asserting yourself with logical thinking in an active energy of *doing*.

To know if you're more comfortable in your masculine or feminine embodiment, spend some time with yourself and tune into how you physically feel. Does taking charge and making decisions fuel or drain your energy? Does adapting to change and going with the flow of life make you feel peaceful or anxious?

Sometimes, our masculine and feminine energies are influenced by our external circumstances. Let's take a look at some examples of each and how our experiences can create blocks or distortions, making it a little confusing to determine which feels most natural to us:

Lily's a single mother, a core feminine energy, and the sole provider for her household. Her daily life is structured around her job and her children, and she focuses all of her resources on providing for others, often neglecting herself in the process. Because the safety and care of her children are her first priority, she regularly steps into the role of the masculine. However, operating in this energy day in and day out leaves her feeling drained, exhausted, and self-abandoned.

Michael's a creative entrepreneur who has built a lucrative art business from the ground up. He often oscillates between the creative self-expression of his art (feminine) and the day-to-day operations of running a business (masculine). Michael's art recently received some negative feedback, affecting his self-esteem. He no longer feels secure in expressing himself for fear of criticism and rejection, and his business is taking a hit. He now spends most of his time finding practical solutions to his financial situation versus embracing his creativity, which was the foundation for his business in the first place.

In these examples above, we see how two individuals, who initially identify as core feminine energies, regularly turn to their inner masculine and overcompensate to "get the job done." Now imagine if Lily had support to ease some of the burdens of responsibility from her shoulders. By moving into a more nurturing role as a caretaker for her children, she could create a more natural flow of energy in the home and in herself. In Michael's case, feeling safe, secure, and emotionally supported in his self-expression would build his self-esteem to such a degree that criticism and rejection would be only a minor hindrance. He could continue in his natural creative state, which only helps his business to thrive.

Let's look at an example for the masculine:

John's a new father and a core masculine energy, but because his wife earns more money at her job, they've mutually decided she would return to work and he would stay home with their newborn. His once-structured day has become increasingly dependent on his ability to be flexible according to his child's needs, and where he once identified as a financial provider for his household, he now struggles to figure out his role as an active participant in his family. As a result, he finds himself becoming more passive in his approach to life and regularly retreats inwardly.

Laura is John's wife, who has a successful career as a corporate strategist. Because she maintains a higher income and loves her work, it was mutually decided she would return to her job while her husband stays home with their child. Working in a corporate setting of structure and routine isn't conducive to Laura's natural feminine energy of flow and surrender, and she often suppresses her intuition in favor of the working, logical mind. As a result, she finds herself stepping more into her masculine energy to assert herself as a leader in her field.

It's important to recognize that masculine and feminine energies don't have to conform to traditional gender roles. Particularly in John and Laura's example, men can thrive as primary caretakers for their children just as women can be best suited for working in a corporate setting. What we're looking at is the dominant *energy* versus the external situation.

If John, as a core masculine, can create some stability in routine, take on the responsibilities of the home, and find a sense of self-identity as a provider for the physical care versus the financial needs of his family, he can successfully remain anchored in his natural masculine energy in this new role. Similarly, Laura, owning her natural feminine energy, can create a work environment that's receptive to open communication and guided by intuition, enabling her to thrive in bringing landmark ideas and creative solutions to her clients.

These are all acute examples to showcase how our experiences, our environments, and even, in some cases, our wounding and traumas can inform and shift the energy within us. However, recognizing and embracing our core energy allows us to succeed no matter the external circumstances.

Through societal programming, we're conditioned to believe one archetype is better, making us feel we have to be less than what we are. Take Laura's scenario of working in a corporate setting, for example. Because of the fight for gender equality, many females are forced to step into a masculine energy in order to experience the same success as their male counterparts. They may censor their intuitive abilities and creative expression to fit a more masculine role of rational thinking and a go-getter personality. In Michael's scenario, because emotions have historically been frowned upon in society, many males are taught to stifle their vulnerability and self-expression. In both cases, the feminine energy is suppressed in favor of a masculine-dominant world.

Let's talk more about feminine energy, as the lack of feminine energy—or the presence of distorted feminine energy—is truly an epidemic that's plagued our world, resulting in toxic masculinity and the power struggles we see today.

Throughout your life, you might have felt like you couldn't adequately express yourself. People talked over you or shut you down or criticized and judged you, and so you hid yourself away, abandoning that crucial part of yourself. You weren't allowed to express your creativity as your full authentic self. You didn't feel safe to surrender and simply be in a world that constantly had you on your guard. You couldn't receive because you were in constant giving mode—giving of your material goods, giving of yourself, giving of your very essence.

(I see you. I understand. I've been there, too.)

These experiences created a polarity flip wherein you felt forced to step into your masculine energy. You adopted a prideful "I can do it all myself" attitude and became self-sufficient— perhaps to the point of hyper-independence. Independence is a beautiful, empowering, and even necessary trait; however, within the polarity flip, this independent energy becomes distorted and stems from lack versus security. You can do it because you've been pushed into that role. You can do it because it's been proven through your experiences that no one will do it for you. You can do it because you have to.

When I was ill in the early years of my struggle with Lyme disease, I experienced this for myself. I owned my home, cared for my animals, and maintained a good and stable job that I liked well enough. Yet, over the course of six months after a routine gallbladder surgery, I found my health rapidly declining. I was unable to walk without support, my heart was weakening, and I was in steady cognitive decline. Even after a proper diagnosis, which took months and concluded fifteen years of misdiagnosis and medical mystery, it would be years before I was close to functioning. I spent most of my time bedridden, struggling to make meals or even dress myself. Still, I forced myself to go to work as often as possible, stubbornly rejecting outside help. I was in both an over-masculine energy ("I can do it all myself") and a distorted feminine energy, feeling powerless to this illness. It was only when I relapsed that I allowed myself to fully surrender to my circumstances. I quit my corporate job to focus on my health and allowed myself to receive financial support from family, friends, and local assistance programs. I was beginning to shift out of the masculine energy I'd become accustomed to.

When we suppress our inner feminine energy, we over-compensate with masculine energy as a form of protection and self-preservation. Our masculine energy makes us feel safe in a world that, quite frankly, doesn't. Humbling myself to accept support was the first step in a long journey of reconnecting to and expressing my Divine Feminine essence.

Both the lack of feminine energy and the distorted feminine energy isn't just experienced by females. It's also seen in males or those who embody core masculine energy. Again, because of societal programming, we have generations of men who were raised to believe they have to stifle their emotions—it's the "real men don't cry" toxic tagline. This suppression of feminine energy leads to a hyper-masculinity in men, creating a power dynamic of control, dominance, and combativeness. This is where aggression, insta-bility, and corruption of self and others can be seen. Additionally, a lack of *healthy* feminine energy in men can also lead to passivity, emotional immaturity, and feelings of inherent weakness.

In both examples, the feminine principle is suppressed or distorted. Do we see then the importance of feminine energy? In females or those who resonate as core feminine, the recognition and acceptance of their feminine energy brings them to their natural state, which heals. In males or those who resonate as core mascu-line, honoring of the feminine energy balances out the masculine, which creates peace. Both are necessary to operate in a harmonized world.

The world as we've known it doesn't make room for us to be who we truly are. Instead, it tries to mold us into fixed versions of who it assumes us to be, stripping away authenticity and creating an energetic war between the masculine and feminine energies.

That war is over.

This is what we're here to change through our union with ourselves and in conscious connections with others.

What Does Distorted Energy Mean?

In our world of duality, we have both the shadow and the light, the wounded and the healed, the unconscious and the conscious. When looking at masculine and feminine energy, we continue to see these polarities in the *distorted* masculine and feminine energies and the *divine* masculine and feminine energies. The terms Divine Masculine and Divine Feminine, as we'll refer to them going forward, can also be reflected in the moniker "sacred" or "conscious" in that we're looking at the healed aspects verses the wounded nature of each energy.

The distorted or wounded energy is the unconscious or unhealed self. This is the shadow self and the level of consciousness from which the majority of our world operates. Throughout our ascension journey, we learn how to clear and heal these distortions to recognize our true nature as divine beings. When we listed the traits of the masculine and feminine in the previous diagram, we were looking at the divine essence. Falling into extremes, the lens gets muddled, and that essence becomes distorted. In our unconscious states, we seem to get further and further away from our divine being, causing confusion, imbalance, and disharmony in ourselves, which then reflects in our relationships and experiences.

For example, the distorted masculine is aggressive versus assertive, chaotic versus disciplined, and controlling versus directive. He might be avoidant or dominating instead of a peaceable leader, or critical and confrontational instead of supportive and protective. The distorted feminine is withholding versus nurturing, codependent versus co-creative, and manipulating versus surrendered to a natural state of ease and flow. She might revel in victimhood or feelings of helplessness—this is the "damsel in distress" archetype that may give way to insecurity, emotional instability, and anxiousness.

Here's a chart to further depict the shadows or distortions of the masculine and feminine energies:

Distorted Masculine Energy	Distorted Feminine Energy
Dominating	Clinging
Calculating	Smothering
Withdrawn	Needy
Possessive	Co-dependent
Jealous	Insecure
Blaming	Victimhood
Irresponsible	Powerless
Aggressive	Overly Emotional
Manipulating	Manipulating
Undisciplined	Inauthentic
Reactive	Weakness
Avoidant	Lazy
Unstable	Withholding
Confrontational	Compromising Values

These traits aren't a judgment, and please don't identify with them as a personal attack or shortcoming. These traits are a result of the programming we've all succumbed to at some point in our lives as part of the unconscious self, living in an unconscious world.

Through our increasing awareness, our job is to heal and clear away these distortions, remembering they're just a reflection of society's conditioning based on limiting beliefs and old templates. Who we truly are as soul is the divine essence, and the more we remember this divine essence, the more we create a new conscious self in the wholeness of both polarities.

Let's summarize all of this. You, yourself, who are reading these words, contain both masculine and feminine principles within your energy. All of the masculine and feminine traits apply, but you also have a core essence wherein you'll relate to and feel more at home in one or the other. You might also recognize times when your masculine and/or feminine energies are acting out of a wounded or distorted state. Again, this isn't a judgment, as this is happening unconsciously. However, the more conscious you become, the more you're accountable for changing your beliefs or mindsets that led to the unconscious pattern. This shift then leads to the embodiment of your Divine Masculine or Divine Feminine energy, and the healed state of the two in balance becomes your inner union.

THE TWIN FLAME

When you meet your Twin Flame, you're encountering yourself energetically in another physical person. You can refer to this soul connection as Twin Flames, sacred partners, or divine counterparts, or you can apply these teachings to any conscious connection. Remember: the label really doesn't matter because, spiritually, there is no other. Everyone you meet is an aspect of you in some way, as nothing is outside of you—not the darkness, not the light. Not the world, not the Universe. Not your beloved. We're all fragments of the one Divine Mother-Father Source, and everyone you encounter is a part of you as you're a part of them.

Alfred, Lord Tennyson once wrote in his poem, *Ulysses*, "I am a part of all I have met." I've carried this line in my heart since I read it nearly 25 years ago, but I didn't fully understand it as a depiction of oneness until my ascension. This, too, is the grace of our ascension journey—for all we know, there's always more to know, with greater understanding and deeper meaning.

We're past versions, present versions, and future versions of each other. Shadowed versions and light versions, we're all part of each other, having our unique experiences with our unique personalities, reflecting these unique aspects of ourselves to ourselves. When we really put this into perspective, how can we not love each other!

Then there's the beloved, the sacred partner. Your Twin Flame catalyzes you to this journey of growth and expansion by showing you yourself as yourself. You're two parts to the one whole—the masculine and feminine polarity embodied as physical partners—and as such, they're your greatest mirror in which you recognize all aspects of yourself across all timelines.

When I was activated to my ascension journey with my counterpart, it was a crash course in further healing. Suddenly, I was being energetically pushed to keep my heart open and trust my inner guidance, to surrender to his masculine presence, and to allow myself to become vulnerably expressive in the safety of his energy. I healed, too, my inner masculine—recognizing my ability to find that security within myself, discovering the inner strength to establish boundaries and the courage to be assertive and decisive.

Recently, when I was on the plane to England as part of a spiritual pilgrimage for my 40th birthday, I sat in quiet contemplation of where this sacred union path had brought me so far. This trip would be an integration of everything I had learned and experienced along this journey, and I was beginning to anchor in the knowledge of my inner masculine now as a sacred embodiment. That is, I was *really* beginning to connect to and feel my counterpart energy as my own inner masculine and not something or someone outside of myself. I knew this intellectually—I've especially felt this in phases along my journey—but to experience this as a consistent, natural feeling was something altogether new for me.

In the sacred temple of the White Spring, the masculine counterpart to the Chalice Well garden in Glastonbury, I felt this internal shift. We approached down a set of stone steps into a musky, candlelit cavern, a bathing pool attached to the spring in its center and little alcoves with altars along the perimeter. I was drawn to the back of the cavern, where there was a small altar adorned with crystals, candles, burning frankincense, and a statue of the Celtic god, Cernunnos. I sat on a little wooden bench directly in front of it, allowing my heart to open while I focused on the flickering flames of the tea candles. The energy of The White Spring felt heavy—heavier than Chalice Well, at least—but not in a negative way. It felt more grounded, more earthly, more present. I could immediately sense the masculine energy in a way I've only experienced in meditations or channeling. This wasn't just the Divine Masculine or even the Conscious Masculine as I've known it.

"This is the Sacred Masculine."

Hearing those words in my heart, I began to sob. I felt them filter into the very core of my being as its loving presence surrounded me, protecting and honoring me. This presence wasn't in attachment or memory of a physical person, but it was an energy I've always connected to, a love I've experienced since long before I was aware of this journey, long before I had the words.

Around 2014, I attended a past-life regression meditation as part of a spiritual development class. In the meditation, we were guided to an old theater where we were asked to choose an outfit and then wait on the stage to see who came to greet us. Presumably, the outfit we chose was to prepare us for the past-life journey, but stubborn soul that I am, I guess, I bypassed the rack of clothes and sat on a stone bench in the middle of the spotlit stage. The curtains parted, and a tall man came out, did a little jig to make me laugh, and sat on the bench beside me. I rested my head on his shoulder. We didn't speak for the whole of the session. When the meditation was over, I burst into tears, overwhelmed by the jumble of emotions flooding my heart, a pure love I've only glimpsed in this lifetime now lingering as a memory.

Years later, a few months after meeting my counterpart, I attended a group meditation hosted by the same mentor. Once again, we were guided to the theater. Once again, I sat on the bench in my street clothes. Once again, the curtains parted, and once again, I began to cry. It was instant recognition—the same man, the same love.

"Where have you been?" I asked him.

"I never left you," he assured me.

Throughout my spiritual pilgrimage to Europe, the sacred masculine was there, not as a person or a projection or a reflection, but as this ever-loving presence that has always been with me as part of me. This integration was the beginning stages of my embodiment of the divine union within.

Twin Flames & Shared Energy

We've already established that you have both masculine and feminine energies within you, but this can't be emphasized enough, especially when it comes to understanding Twin Flames. It's easy to look at your physical counterpart and think of them as separate from yourself. Of course it is—they're a whole other person! Naturally, when we interact, our human minds see them as the external counterpart, classifying them as, "my Divine Masculine" or "my Divine Feminine." But again, the energy of the Divine Masculine or Divine Feminine they're embodying is also within you. That's the crux of these Twin Flame connections—they *are* you within another physical form.

To put it simply: the energy of your physical Divine Masculine is also the energy of *your inner masculine*. The energy of your physical Divine Feminine is also *your inner feminine*. Union is the recognition of this oneness within you.

I'm getting ahead of myself. We'll touch much more on this later.

Twin Flames, being one energy split into two physical bodies, share a chakra system. While all chakras have both yin (feminine) and yang (masculine) energies, as it relates to the purpose of Twin Flames, it was shown to me as follows:

The feminine energy resides in the upper three chakras—the crown, the brow or third eye, and the throat chakras. She's connected to higher power, her intuition, and her self-expression. She sees things from the energetic or soul's perspective, giving her a wide-eyed lens of life and her spiritual journey. This is why the Divine Feminine is considered to "awaken" to conscious recognition of this connection first.

The masculine energy resides in the lower three chakras—the root, the sacral, and the solar plexus chakras. He's connected to the earth and material form, is a stable and present energetic container, and is assertive and courageous when moved to action. Whereas the feminine energy brings the wisdom, insight, and ideas of spiritual essence down, the masculine grounds this into the physical world with structure, discipline, and movement.

I once channeled the beautiful message between counterparts, "Meet me on the bridge of the heart." As the masculine energy rises from the lower chakras and the feminine energy descends through the higher chakras, balance is created on this bridge of the heart chakra. The heart is a generator for energy. It's here your connection has and always will exist, and it's here you co-create and give birth to new energetic realities.

Say you want to build a house. The feminine energy will first have the idea—she'll imagine the blueprint, envision how many doors and windows it has, and visualize paint colors and furniture for the rooms. The masculine energy will bring this into tangible form by hiring a contractor or even building the house himself. It's in this harmony of the two that the vision of the house is birthed into being.

You do this every single day in your individual life, and the more you come into balance within yourself, the more fluidly these manifestations take shape. This is your alignment, your inner union. In conscious connections, this is seen in working harmony with your significant other. Perhaps it's an idea for a date night your partner puts into action, or the actual creation of a family, business, or home. Whether in physical relationship or your own inner energy, masculine and feminine are always creating together.

UNITING THE MASCULINE & FEMININE

The masculine and feminine energies always want to be in harmony with each other. We see this occurring effortlessly in nature where the feminine is the life-force while the masculine is the powerful, grounding presence.

A few years ago, I was with one of my soul sisters in upstate New York visiting the many scenic waterfalls and national parks. As we paused to admire the view from an overlook, she remarked how the waterfall reminded her of the masculine and the feminine. I was blown away—it's such a perfect example of the masculine and feminine working in harmony in nature!

The water is the feminine energy moving freely, even wildly, while the rocks over which the water cascades represent the masculine energy of structure and discipline, providing a container of safety for the feminine to flow in full expression of herself. Without the container of the embankment, the ground would flood—just as the feminine's emotions would flood within the human vessel without the energetic container of the masculine. We see this in emotional instability or immaturity. With the masculine's leadership and presence, however, there's a sense of direction for where the water—or her emotions—should flow. The masculine container isn't a box to suppress the feminine but rather an energy in which she's divinely held and supported.

In a sacred relationship, both the Divine Masculine and Divine Feminine counterparts serve as mirrors of the inner masculine and feminine energies. Throughout your journey, the polarities will switch and the roles will reverse, depending on what's being healed. For example, you might find yourself, a core Divine Feminine, stepping more into your inner masculine energy as you work on your material world while your counterpart, a core Divine Masculine, operates more in their inner feminine energy to connect to their intuition or heal their self-expression.

Generally, the masculine counterpart shows the Divine Feminine how to heal her mind—to silence the chatter, clear the old beliefs, and release the negative thought patterns, creating a consciousness shift that aligns her with her true soul self. The feminine counterpart then shows the Divine Masculine how to trust his intuition, follow his heart, and express his emotions. It's here you teach each other, bringing the unconscious to light. It's here balance is restored.

Every intimate relationship is showing us something about ourselves. Every connection is a catalyst for our growth. This is the beauty of sacred relationships. When we allow ourselves to see the mirror and consciously do the work, greater healing of ourselves and our world is possible.

POEM
FOR THE
DIVINE FEMININE

She's the combined goddess
of the compassionate warrior
housed within the temple
of everything I was,
everything I am,
everything
I'm about to become.

(Fierce. Formidable.
Tender. True.)

I've traveled lifetimes
to recognize myself
as I do now—
diving into the ancient
catacombs of my heart,
navigating the universal
pathways of my soul,
dying a thousand times
in a thousand moments
to come alive again
and again
and again.

(Reborn,
my feminine rises.)

I've sacrificed myself
to the world—

stifling my voice,
suppressing all emotions,
hiding from my eternal light.

(No more,
I shatter the silence.)

The world pushes back,
shouting outraged contradictions:
"You're not enough!"
"You're too much!"
"Be more!"
"Become less!"

It chips away at me,
creates cratered scars
where love is meant to mend,
not bleed.

(Who did you want me to be?)

I cut these strings
and dive into the core
of my faithful truth,
swimming
through the wild unknown
to claim pieces
of my neglected self,
getting lost and found
and still here I am.

(Here I still am.)

The world tries to smother
the holy flame.
Don't you know
I'm a phoenix
and the embers
are my domain?

Brought to my knees
through a thousand surrenders
I grow stronger
and softer
all at once.

(This is my gift,
my humble offering.)

I'm setting fire to the lies
of all I've been told
and breaking loose
from the shackles
of my existence.

(In this space,
I am the beloved.
In this place,
I am part of the sacred.)

I'm ready to dance
in the wilderness
of all that I am.

(In this moment
I become.)

I set my feminine free.

CHAPTER THREE
THE EVOLUTION OF TWIN FLAMES

"So, I love you because the entire Universe
conspired to help me find you."
– Paulo Coehlo, *The Alchemist*

WHEN I MET MY COUNTERPART for our first coffee date in 2016, we were two former classmates catching up—or so I thought. I didn't know we'd meet again a year later and our journey would unfold from there. I didn't know I'd unlock my guarded heart and open to the most profound possibilities of unconditional love I could ever experience. I didn't know I'd be launched on an exploration of my very soul in what would be the greatest challenge and the best adventure of my life.

On that early evening at the local diner, I only knew we were old friends sitting in a booth across from each other. I could feel my body vibrating, but I didn't understand why.

Looking back now, I can see something was beginning to activate. From an energetic standpoint, we were meant to come together, but our chakra systems weren't yet aligned to the point that we were ready to reunite for our ascension, and I was feeling the difference in frequency. We would still have more of our individual journeys to experience.

Chinese culture has a beautiful myth called the Red Thread of Fate, commonly known today as the Invisible String Theory, where an invisible red cord is wrapped around the fingers of those destined to meet. When I look back on my journey, I can see how the thread of us was entwined right from the start and that it would continue to weave a tapestry throughout our lives.

We parted ways that evening at the entrance to the diner with a hug and a promise to keep in touch, and we both kept that promise. Over the next year, we shared memes and messages, reaching out to each other as a catch-up every few months. I spent my year confronting difficult experiences that I can recognize now were preparing me for my ascension journey, though, of course, I didn't know that either at the time. My grandmother had a stroke and was moved into assisted living, and I was there to support my parents as we cleaned and arranged her house for sale—a house that had been an intrinsic part of my upbringing. Saying goodbye to that house felt like saying goodbye to a piece of my childhood, and I spent time grieving the loss and learning to let go.

During that time, I was also working on healing my physical and emotional body after a relapse from Lyme disease, and rather than repeating cycles of the past where I resisted the inevitable changes that came with illness, I was finally learning to surrender. I focused on nurturing myself and building back my self-esteem and sense of purpose in the world. I also began slowly healing my fractured relationship with God.

By 2017, I had founded a non-profit to provide hope and healing to Lyme patients struggling with the emotional toll of chronic illness—something that has always been near and dear to my heart and the essence of which I've infused even into my work at *Susan Dawn Spiritual Connections*. I'd also published my novel, *The Last Letter*, several months earlier and was promoting it at Lyme conferences and speaking events as part of advocacy efforts. In July, determined to keep healing and changing my life for the better after years of suffering, I posted to my friends and family that I was seeking resources for manifesting the positive in life, "all woo-woo spirituality stuff welcomed!" In early September, I completed my first Reiki course—something, I would later find out, my counterpart also did and with the same teacher! Unknowingly, the dots were beginning to connect.

Back in the spring of 2017, I casually shared on my social media that I wanted to see the new Broadway adaptation of the musical, *Anastasia.* By the end of September, I was on a train to New York to spend my birthday weekend with one of my best friends, who was flying in from Chicago. This was a huge step for me. It was the first time I'd traveled for pleasure since I'd been sick, and the energy of the city boosted my confidence, resolve, and sense of independence again. We giggled as we recounted the magic of an evening spent manifesting pictures with the actors at the stage door, and we shared deep soul conversations about spiritual concepts as we wandered the gardens at The Met Cloisters. At one point, she talked about Twin Flames, but it was like a veil had fallen over my mind—I was blocked from understanding what was being said. When I returned home, a friend commented that he'd never seen me so happy. I realized I hadn't felt like this—truly like myself—in years.

A little less than two months later, as I was feeling a stark, uplifting change in the energy within myself, my counterpart reached out to meet for coffee. We had to cancel plans the night before, but he was quick to reschedule for the next evening, November 22—my grandmother's birthday and the night before Thanksgiving. I arrived at the diner first and was waiting by the hostess counter, turning around just as he reached for the first set of doors. Our eyes met, and our faces lit up with smiles. For the next two hours, it felt like time stopped and we were alone in a magical, sacred bubble.

This is the Twin Flame activation. It's not something that's sought, but rather, it's something that's experienced in what's known as divine timing, when the energy centers are aligned and the first soul merge occurs. This initial meeting is the start of your ascension journey—a deeper level of spiritual awakening wherein you're returning home to your true essence of unconditional love and oneness.

Now, I know what it sounds like, and this is where the journey can be so misconstrued. Because there's so much love in essentially a "love at first sight" experience, we think this is the classic depiction of fairytale romance. Your sacred union *is* a love story, but it's also so much more than that, and it's only in surrendering to the depths of this journey that we begin to unlock the true purpose of such a sacred relationship.

THE TWIN FLAME JOURNEY

A new cycle is activated when you meet your Twin Flame, known colloquially as the Twin Flame Journey. It's given this name because, for all intents and purposes, it *is* a journey—one that leads you on a new path, a path of the soul. While the Twin Flame experience seems to follow certain "stages" as a basic blueprint within a collective energy—and within that collective, there may also be various segments that feel energetically familiar—it's important to remember that your journey is yours. *You* write the blueprint. *You* set the path. You can shift your energy and change the course of your journey at any moment.

This journey can feel overwhelming for all the challenges we experience as we're clearing the old templates, but it's not intended to create havoc and chaos in your life—though our human minds can certainly perceive it this way! It's to accelerate your ascension and align you with your soul, which has its own particular blueprint to follow.

Please don't compare your journey to another's—you're never ahead or behind what's meant for you. Understanding the collective energies and what others are experiencing can be incredibly helpful for navigating this journey, but your journey is perfectly yours. The more you can allow for your journey to unfold, the more successful you'll be.

These experiences, or so-called "stages," of the Twin Flame Journey can happen at different times, in different orders, and even not at all. Here's a typical blueprint that many within the collective experience:

+ The Meeting/Activation
+ Honeymoon
+ Triggers & Challenges
+ Separation
+ Inner Union
+ Physical Union

Now, I want to emphasize that there really is no blueprint—at least, not one you need to adhere to. There is a collective experience, and that's where having this awareness can be helpful, but your journey is yours and only yours. You're not failing or messing up or doing your journey "wrong" or "right" if you experience any of this differently than what's presented. It's simply meant as guidance as you continue along your ascension path. Once you reach a certain point in your ascension, you'll be so in tune with yourself that you'll be trusting your path no matter what "stage" you're "supposed" to be in.

It simply won't matter.

But we'll share more on that later. For now, we're going to continue with the journey as we *think* we know it…

Let's break the journey down into each specific stage.

ACTIVATING YOUR ASCENSION

Prior to uniting with your counterpart, you'll likely experience an energetic upgrade in your life—unconsciously feeling some kind of renewal, a greater sense of purpose or new self-confidence, or even an anticipation of some exciting change just on the horizon. You've been leveling up in some way, and this joyous energy is preparing you for your soul's reunion with your Twin Flame.

It had been a few months since my counterpart and I checked in to say hi to each other as we'd been doing most of that year in 2017, and for nearly two months leading up to our November reunion at the diner, I found myself repeatedly singing the lyrics, "I don't know when, I don't know how, but I know something's starting right now," from Disney's *The Little Mermaid*. I could sense something coming, but I had no idea what it was. Never in my wildest dreams could I imagine the journey that was to unfold.

Even as a fairly descriptive writer, it's hard to put this experience into human terms. Plato does a pretty good job when he says, "And so, when a person meets the half that is his very own... then something wonderful happens: the two are struck from their senses by love, by a sense of belonging to one another, and by desire, and they don't want to be separated from one another, not even for a moment."

At the time of your ascension activation, even if you've known each other before, you'll experience a spark of familiarity with your Twin Flame called soul recognition. This usually occurs through eye contact, though this can also happen through hearing each other's voice. It feels as if you've known each other forever, for lifetimes—like no time or space or distance has ever separated you. It feels as if you're looking at a part of yourself you didn't even know was missing, but once your eyes meet or you hear their voice, you realize how empty you've felt and how whole you've always been all at once. Time stops. You might feel an energetic pulse within your body. It's as if you're the only two people in the world, even in all of existence, as you enter into what can only be described as a sacred bubble.

It feels like you've come home.

Through your individual journeys, your frequencies have been rising to such a point that you're able to enter into the vortex of each other's energy. Now, in the physical contact of your meeting, your shared chakra system aligns. This is what activates your ascension.

As we left the diner that evening, I turned to my counterpart, prepared to say goodbye and part again as old classmates like we had done the year before, even though I could intuitively sense this was altogether something new, something more. Instead, he walked me to my car where we lingered a while longer, both reluctant to leave. When I finally got in my car, grinning like an idiot, I screamed to the Universe, "What the hell just happened?!" and drove home like I was traveling on a cloud.

I called my best friend, doing my best to explain how something in my heart flipped—like he woke me up, like I was home. No matter how this went, I told her, I could tell something important was happening, something worthwhile, something that was speaking to the very core of my being.

My friend was silent as I talked. Then she said thoughtfully, "I think you just met your Twin Flame."

Twin Flame. A phrase I hadn't consciously heard before and never would have considered if it weren't for the stirrings of truth within my soul. I wanted to deny this, to box it in and say, "He's just an old classmate; we're just friends"—and I probably did at first! But the more I tried to restrict myself, the more my soul seemed to protest.

Soon after your initial meeting, you'll begin to see synchronicities—repeating numbers known as Angel Numbers or symbols and signs that speak to you. You might see your counterpart's name or initials in the most unlikely of places like billboards, sports jerseys, and license plates, or you'll consistently drive past the same make and model of their car. You might even see certain animals or objects you've come to attribute to them. Once, when I was struggling in the beginning stages of my journey, I broke open a fortune cookie to read the words "in union, there is strength" written on the tiny slip of paper. Okay, Universe. We read you loud and clear!

These signs and synchronicities are the Universe communicating with you, and the more conscious you become, the more easily you can interpret what's being shown to you.

Music is a common synchronicity. You might suddenly tune into a song playing in the grocery store that holds significance or turn to a random radio station only to hear lyrics matching your experience. For those open to their intuitive gifts, you'll even get music "downloads" in which a song suddenly pops into your mind carrying some kind of meaningful message. This is often experienced as telepathy between Twin Flames.

The further along on our journey we go, the more our psychic or intuitive gifts begin to open. For some, this could be a jarring experience of sudden visions or inner knowing, energy pulses, or lucid dreams. For others who have been on a spiritual path for a while, the expansion of your gifts may seem more fluid. For myself, since I've always been an intuitive person and had already been on a spiritual journey for many years, this activation led to a deepening of trust within myself and a newfound *conscious* awareness of my gifts and the universal energies that I'd felt but couldn't yet articulate. It was like I had pieces of a puzzle, and my ascension, with the help of my counterpart, began to put the pieces of that puzzle into place.

Even while my activation was a little more subtle, thanks to my previous spiritual studies and levels of awakening, I soon began to experience phenomena that made me question my own sanity. I could feel my counterpart's energy as if he were in the room beside me, and at times, I could smell his distinctly pleasant aroma, like he had just walked in the door. I even woke up from a sound sleep one morning because I could audibly hear his voice even though he was miles away. On one occasion, I was working at my desk when I felt the strange sensation I was seeing out of his eyes, and I ran to the bathroom mirror to make sure my eyes were still brown, not blue. Even my counterpart once admitted to experiencing phenomenon, saying time seemed to stand still whenever we were together.

Everyone's personal experiences with Twin Flame telepathy will look a little different, and it will certainly make you question your reality; however, this, too, is the meaning of ascension. It's a shift from perceiving one's physical reality as the only reality to understanding there's so much more yet unseen.

I feel incredibly grateful that I had my best friends and soul sisters by my side from the very beginning. They were a true grounding force, and the fact that they reflected my journey in their own spiritual experiences was validating as my ascension took turn after turn, with challenge after challenge and miracle after miracle.

One such soul sister was my best friend from Chicago, whom I had met ten years prior as part of the same blogging community where we became fast friends as fellow novelists. Over the years, we created projects together and encouraged each other's writing work, our bond growing more profound during our trip to New York as our individual spiritual journeys created another link in our deepening friendship. She was the one who initially pointed me to the concept of Twin Flames, and I imagine without her, I'd still be trying to put a powerfully spiritual connection into a limiting box!

Another significant soul sister was someone I'd met through the Lyme disease community, and through sharing our stories and our struggles, we grew infinitely closer. It was only when she revealed what was happening within a new relationship that I realized we, too, were reflecting the same experiences, and while she doesn't affix to the Twin Flame label, her journey is remarkably parallel in that we'll catch up only to discover we're having similar encounters with our respective partners. It's been both refreshing and confirming of my own journey to have someone not part of the "Twin Flame collective"—who doesn't pay attention to readings or energy updates but who has done her inner healing work through learning about conscious connections—show me that the experience, no matter what label is placed on it or what path is walked, is very real.

I've had the absolute honor of meeting others along my journey, including many clients-turned-soul family with whom I've formed an enduring bond. Others, still, will join us at certain stages, though they might not remain in our physical reality for long. The depth and duration of these connections boil down to energetic compatibility as we continue our individual ascension, but each one is invaluable for the wisdom they offer and the lessons they reflect.

This is the importance of community. Especially for those who resonate as the core Divine Feminine, one of the greatest challenges of our ascension is discerning between ego and intuition. Our journey teaches us to trust our inner experience over what's presented in our physical reality. Community provides a sacred space where we can explore and integrate this newfound level of personal trust.

Following gallbladder surgery in the fall of 2011, my health began to decline rapidly. I was having trouble maintaining my balance and clinging to walls for support; I was having heart palpitations and fainting, and I was losing my cognitive ability. There were periods when I couldn't read the documents on a computer screen, couldn't recognize one of my best friends when she was standing right in front of me, and couldn't remember even the most common words. I was in the ER at least once a week, seeing specialist after specialist, and even had a neurology appointment with one of the top teaching hospitals in the country. Every doctor assured me there was nothing wrong, diagnosed me with something relatively mild like a vitamin deficiency or anxiety, and sent me on my way.

Meanwhile, I was getting worse. I was sleeping eighteen hours a day, unable to even lift my head from the pillow to check the time on my bedside clock, and at one point, my mom and I compiled a list of over forty symptoms I was experiencing at any given moment. My skin was constantly grey and pale, the light in my eyes had gone out, and my usually bubbly personality was a memory. I'd become a ghost of my former self.

Something was very, very wrong.

Six months later, on a warm May afternoon in 2012, I sat with my parents in a doctor's office two and a half hours away from home, crying with relief as a Lyme specialist validated my symptoms and gave me hope for healing. If I had listened to those doctors who dismissed me so readily, if I had disregarded my intuition that told me there was something more going on with my health than they were able to detect through all their tests and procedures, if I had accepted someone's word over my truth and didn't advocate for myself, I wouldn't be here today.

Such is the significance, I learned, of trusting oneself. Such is the necessity of not giving up on yourself and what you know in your soul to be true when the world feels like it's against you. Such is the value of having community—like I had my family to support me, like I had my doctor who believed me, like I had the Lyme community who shared their stories, which helped me confirm my intuition and saved my life.

Having this situation as a foundation for my ascension was a blessing, as it showed me how to rely on and trust my intuition from the earliest stages. Along my journey, I've had several people step in as presumed soul family, only for them to negate my experiences, try to influence my spiritual path, and attempt to make me doubt my own counterpart connection. One individual even confidently declared that someone she'd just met was my Twin Flame and that I should give up my counterpart. I didn't care about the labels; I cared about the person, the soul of the individual I was interacting with daily, and the absurdity of such a statement quickly helped me see the situation for what it was—a lesson in discernment. I honored myself and my soul's guidance and immediately disengaged from further interaction, continuing my journey without her.

No guide, guru, friend, psychic, or teacher can ever tell you the truth of your experience and your inner knowing—it's something you discover and hold sacred within yourself. However, having a community supporting your growth helps you feel not so alone on what can be an incredibly challenging and lonely road home to yourself.

And we're not meant to walk alone.

Okay, let's back up again... Let's talk about feeling crazy along this journey for a minute because it's true: this journey is batshit bananas. You're dismantling everything you once believed and everything you thought you knew. You're looking at the world with fresh eyes, like you've just been reborn, and it's all so exciting but also raw and vulnerable. Your heart is expanding, and you're feeling more than you ever thought possible. At the same time, your mind is opening to new concepts and ideas that you'd never considered or that once seemed impossible, and you're having personal experiences with all of it that make you question and doubt everything.

Good. The questions and doubt are the start of a journey to discovering that the answers are always within you, and they'll come up again and again as you're asked to turn your focus away from what you think you know logically to tune into your inner knowing, your soul's truth.

Think of it like this: on the surface, a book is just a book. But in your hands, you're also holding atoms bonding and vibrating at such specific speeds that they become tangible. Now look at these letters on the page—they're just ink on a sheet of paper, right? Yet combined in such a way, they create words, which make a sentence, which translates a thought, tells a story, and evokes a feeling or sensation within you.

If that's not magic, I don't know what is!

Such is the fabric of the Universe. Prior to our awakening, we might look at our physical reality as surface-level and simplistic—we have a house, a family, and a job. However, the more our spiritual perception expands, the more we understand that reality is so much more than what's experienced on the surface. Energy is moving through everything, and we're constantly creating with that energy. Someone had to have the idea for the house in order to build it, and many scenarios may have had to align in order for that house to become yours. That alignment, too, is energy.

So, we begin to understand there's more going on energetically when it comes to our reality, and this extends to our relationships, wherein we also recognize the energy beneath our connections. Our connection with our counterpart along our sacred journey is the strongest catalyst for this change in perception, as it's also the strongest connection we have. As you start seeing signs and synchronicities drawing you towards each other, you might doubt what you're experiencing because you're still trying to put it in a box of old relationship rules. But that doubt is also the initiation for your growth. This spiritual connection is intended to transform you completely.

Welcome to your sacred union path of ascension.

HEARTS IN HARMONY

Upon the initial activation of your journey, you and your counterpart will usually enter a "honeymoon" stage where everything feels blissful while you get to know each other as individuals. You might communicate frequently, go on dates, or even enter an exclusive, committed relationship.

There are two things that are happening in this stage.

Energetically, you're aligning and experiencing the truth of your connection. You and your Twin Flame are the same soul experiencing itself, and in this energy, you're recognizing each other as the harmonious, unconditional love that naturally exists within you.

Physically, on the surface level, you're getting to know each other as two distinct personalities, and from this human perspective, you might still be trying to apply the old template of relationship to what's primarily a soul connection.

When I met my counterpart, I didn't know what Twin Flames were, and even after I learned more about this spiritual bond, I still didn't fully understand what it meant—nor, truly, are we meant to. The sacred union path of ascension is a process of soul evolution that's meant to be lived. Ascension itself is an inner spiral, and the more we evolve, the more we understand through this lived experience.

There's an ancient proverb that says, "No man ever steps in the same river twice, for it's not the same river, and he's not the same man." The river changes, just as you change, and what you didn't know yesterday, you may now know today. Another example is this: You could read the same book or listen to the same song a thousand times throughout your life, but you'll never interpret it the same way. You'll always read the book or listen to that song from the perspective of who you are now, today.

Such is our ascension.

But I digress…

I didn't have the understanding of Twin Flames or this journey that I do now, and I know this, too, will continue to evolve as I evolve. All I knew back then was suddenly, I was feeling love for someone I'd known my whole life but that I didn't know at all, having spent so many years apart. I couldn't understand how there was such a feeling of safety, ease, and home between us, how we were so compatible down to even the most mundane elements such as our favorite comic book characters, and how rather than closing myself off or overthinking as I had in other connections, all I wanted to do was keep my heart open and let my soul, not my head, guide me.

It wasn't long before we began to trigger each other and our honeymoon period transitioned into the healing journey. This is where the journey can become misconstrued. There's so much undeniable love—beyond what you ever thought possible—but it seems to veer from the typical fairytale blueprint we might expect.

I want to remind you that your journey with your Twin Flame isn't meant to be painful. In fact, pain is the furthest thing from what this journey represents. You are love at the core; however, as you reflect love to each other, you also begin to reflect anything that's not love. This is part of your ascension—to heal and release the illusions created by pain to return to love.

The honeymoon stage is often short-lived because you're designed to activate each other for your ascension. This initial stage may last weeks or months, depending on what your soul has orchestrated for your growth. As someone who had already been experiencing deeper levels of spiritual awakening through the catalyst experience of illness and whose counterpart was also spiritually conscious, our own honeymoon stage seemed to last for only a few short weeks.

The end of the honeymoon stage doesn't mean love ceases to exist or you won't have harmony in your connection as part of your journey. It simply means you're getting down to business regarding the purpose of why these soul connections come together—to activate higher levels of love means first clearing any blocks to love. This is where, through the mirroring process, you and your Twin Flame will trigger each other, shining light on the shadows still housed within. These triggers are meant to bring everything that was unconscious to conscious awareness for healing. This is part of your evolutionary, soul growth process.

TRIGGERS, TRIGGERS EVERYWHERE!

Oftentimes, the strength of one counterpart is a *perceived* weakness in the other. For example, your counterpart might be an excellent communicator while you struggle with self-expression. As you see this perceived lack in yourself reflected in your counterpart, you become triggered. The trigger then initiates the healing process to eliminate this false belief and old patterning.

Twin Flames incarnate for soul growth (with a higher-level mission of changing the paradigm, raising the frequency of the planet, and ushering in a new template of the Christ-Sophia Consciousness, but we'll get to that later). When you and your counterpart activate each other to your ascension, you begin a cycle known as the healing journey. This is an energetic purge of anything attached to an old version of yourself or your life.

When I was in recovery from Lyme disease, I learned that the caterpillar in its chrysalis completely breaks down into a goo-like substance, activating different genes until it emerges as the butterfly. Its starting DNA will be the same, but its metamorphosis transforms it into something completely different than what it originally was. This is what we're experiencing on our ascension journey—a breakdown of old habits, beliefs, and identities. The dissolution of the ego, or false ego, occurs because it's no longer needed as we step out of survival mode.

It's similar to getting a whole new wardrobe—you have to clear out your closet of what no longer fits to embrace what does. In this metaphor, you're upgrading to an energetic wardrobe that's tailor-made for you, resulting in more self-esteem, personal empowerment, and self-love. Think about that perfect pair of jeans or your favorite jacket that encourages confidence. Maybe you hold your head a little higher, walk with more purpose, or simply feel more relaxed. That's the makeover energy you're experiencing within yourself, and while it might be a little unnerving at first because you're used to seeing one version of yourself in the mirror, you're ultimately stepping into an energy that feels more authentic and comfortable to your soul.

Triggers are suppressed emotional energy, and when you're triggered, these old energies are brought to your conscious awareness to be acknowledged and cleared, which brings you into greater harmony with yourself and union with another. Triggers are never intentional between sacred partners—they're simply a prompting of old karma, including beliefs, patterns, and trauma that are drawn to the surface to be healed within your natural energy of unconditional love for each other. What challenges the situation is how this often happens while you're still operating from an unconscious state.

Think of your consciousness like a computer program. You've been running Operating System 1.0 for most of your lifetime, and through your growth, you might put patches on specific beliefs, patterns, or behaviors that lead to certain levels of personal development. During your spiritual awakening, you become more aware of those patches and how you've "upgraded." As you're catalyzed to your ascension, however, the patches no longer work as well. They've simply been surface-level fixes to programs still running in the background. On your ascension journey, you're now writing fresh code and experiencing a new operating system altogether.

Let's say you have an underlying belief that you're not worthy, which is showing up in multiple places in your life—you're underpaid at your job, your spouse and children don't seem to appreciate you, you find yourself refusing acts of kindness from your friends, and you have a habit of being self-deprecating. Through a certain level of self-awareness, you decide you don't like feeling this way, and so you set out to make a change. You apply for a higher-paying job, express your feelings to your family, begin to accept gifts with grace and gratitude, and become more mindful of your self-critical thoughts—perhaps you even read self-help books and take courses to guide your development. These are all healthy starting points for changing patterns and behaviors that lead to growth, but they don't get to the root of the issue, and soon you find that despite these changes, you're still feeling elements of unworthiness.

This is because it's not just your physical life that has to change—that's the patchwork—but your *energy*. In getting to the root of the matter and becoming conscious of the limiting belief behind your feelings of self-worth, you're clearing away the old programming so that now, when you make these physical changes, they integrate into a new energetic version of you.

I'll never forget the day my doorbell rang, and I discovered a FedEx package waiting on my front porch. I'd been struggling financially, practically housebound in the throes of illness, and stubbornly refusing support because I didn't feel worthy, too afraid of becoming a burden. A few weeks earlier, I had mentioned in passing to one of my writing groups that some of the keys on my keyboard had stopped working. When I opened the package, I was shocked to find that a fellow writer had sent me a new laptop. I quickly called her up, attempting to refuse because it was too much—I'd never been given a gift like this before.

"Susan," she said gently but firmly, "don't ever diminish someone's love for you by trying to deny how they want to show you that love."

Something clicked with those words. I'd prided myself on being a good friend and a giving person, and here was a humbling realization that others wanted to share their love with me just as much as I did with them. In this gift of friendship was an offering of true wisdom, teaching me the value of receiving with grace. I've been mindful to never block a blessing since.

However, it wasn't until my ascension journey that I began to unwrap the beliefs around *why* I felt like I didn't deserve the gift of her love in the first place.

Healing happens in layers, and just like with computer code, you might find hidden programming where you thought you had previously cleared a belief. Have patience and compassion for yourself and don't be afraid to keep diving deep, as this creates greater breakthroughs and gets easier along the way. We'll talk more about healing in Chapter Six.

As your divine mirror, your Twin Flame is showing you the shadows to direct you back home to your light. Through unintentional triggers, they're guiding you to heal what's been stuck within your subconscious from childhood and past lifetimes, through ancestral trauma and cellular memory, and from societal programs and collective conditioning. These triggers shine a light on where the wounds are. The wounds need to be revealed to be healed.

Although you and your counterpart activate this healing within each other through these triggers—which can feel devastatingly painful to the human aspect—there's always an undercurrent of love, peace, and forgiveness for each other. Indeed, your counterpart energetically urges you to experience more of this unconditional love, peace, and forgiveness for yourself and the world around you.

This is part of the consciousness shift.

SIMULATING SEPARATION

During the healing stage of your journey, you might experience "separation" between you and your Twin Flame. Separation is often experienced in cycles and may last a few days to many years, depending on the counterparts' energetic alignment, which is influenced by their inner work.

While on the surface, certain stages might seem similar as a collective energy, your journey is always designed for your personal ascension, including any phases of separation with your sacred partner. Some counterparts will experience prolonged separation right away, and some will undergo cycles of separation where they come together only to part again in a repeating pattern. Some counterparts will have families and live together, navigating their journey within a physical relationship, and some will experience a mix of scenarios. It all depends on your soul's need for spiritual evolution.

Because my counterpart lived in the neighboring town, our connection was spent in physical proximity with brief, intermittent cycles of separation wherein we were always drawn back together—sometimes seemingly by magic, as if the Universe was guiding us towards each other in some kind of divine orchestration (hint: it was!). Even when external circumstances should have separated us, miracles kept us together as we embarked on our ascension journey. In 2020, we moved in together, and two years later, we entered our first prolonged period of separation, accelerating our individual growth process.

Separation isn't an indication of whether or not you'll come into physical union, and it's in no way a "failure" of your journey. It's merely an experience in which you're *perceiving* being separate from your counterpart—though it's super-hard for the egoic mind to understand this or see it as anything but painful! To the human self, it feels like abandonment, betrayal, rejection, and any other limiting belief creating an energetic block. However, the core wound you're healing is separation itself.

Separation is anywhere you feel, physically or energetically, disconnected from your counterpart. This stems from feeling disconnected from yourself and even from God, which we'll talk about later in its own chapter.

Separation is an opportunity for a further shift in consciousness as the soul evolves to see beyond the illusion. It's a valuable part of your journey, providing an opportunity for individual growth and expansion. In fact, it's through playing out the illusion of separation that you remember you and your counterpart are and always have been in union.

I was shown separation along the sacred union path of ascension as a simple circle. You and your counterpart meet at one point along your life journey, and while it might look and even feel like you're walking your individual paths from the human perspective—with personalized, "separate" experiences to boot—you're still part of the same circle and always have been. Reunion happens through energetic alignment when your paths converge. Many cycles can occur until you're able to energetically sustain your physical union.

Here's another quick visual that might help put separation as an illusion into perspective: imagine you're walking along a path—a path that's yours and no one else's. Other people might join you for a while on similar paths heading in the same direction, but your path is always your own.

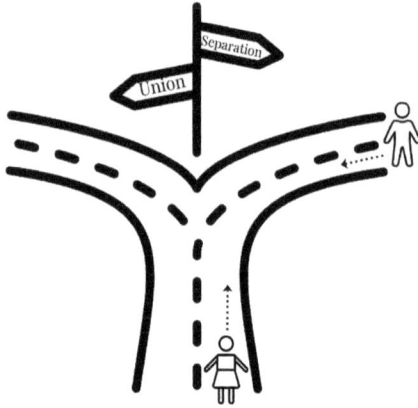

Your counterpart is walking the same exact path because, energetically, your path is their path, too—they're just approaching from the opposite end with different (but parallel) experiences along the way. In the perfect timing, at the most perfect point, you'll converge and create a new branch of the same path, now walking in union. Here you begin to see that despite the perception of separation, you've always been journeying together.

THE MASCULINE & FEMININE PERSPECTIVE

The Divine Masculine and Divine Feminine process their journey in distinct ways, which is why there can be so much confusion and misunderstanding when it comes to the Twin Flame connection. You might be thinking, *wait a minute—if we're one soul, wouldn't we both be experiencing the same thing?* It's a valid question and not a gross reach as far as rational conclusions go, but remember, this journey is an accelerated ascension. How much would you and your counterpart learn if you took the same courses with the same syllabus and the same teachers?

Twin Flames are two parts of the same whole or, as we once channeled, a union of opposites. Beneath the surface, you share the same core lessons, but they'll look unique from the human perspective. For example, one counterpart might experience limitations from an illness, teaching them surrender, while the other might share the same lesson through an injury. The principles of the lesson are the same, but you have different teachers and, thus, different approaches to learning. The same is true for your sacred union journey.

The Divine Feminine experiences the journey from an energetic vantage point. She's known as the more "awakened" counterpart because she consciously understands the connection and the greater purpose of the sacred union path of ascension. She'll be divinely guided to the concept of Twin Flames or sacred relationships teachings and will embark on an inner journey to deconstruct old beliefs and patterns. She might do this through energy clearings, journaling, meditation, self-reflection, or any other spiritually-rooted practice. The Divine Feminine sees the journey from a wider perspective—that is, she sees the bigger picture of the connection and the framework of union as a whole.

The Divine Masculine is more grounded and materially focused with physically-oriented experiences. He, too, goes through a healing process and consciousness shift, but he'll clear karma and transform his beliefs and patterns by first "playing out" experiences in physical form—for example, through karmic relationships or a specific set of circumstances. The Divine Masculine contains his own wisdom, though he might be unaware or untrusting of it, often ignoring his intuition in favor of the logical mind. For some who are further along in their journey, the Divine Masculine might be a highly spiritual individual with a vast understanding of esoteric concepts. But ascension is more than spiritual knowledge—it's a connection to your authentic, sacred self in balance with the heart and the mind. This is why the Divine Masculine is considered the unconscious counterpart until his ascension, where this inner alignment and embodiment take place.

The Divine Feminine sees the whole puzzle picture of their ascension journey, even if she doesn't have all of the pieces just yet. This stems from an intuitive knowing wherein she's guided to trust that she'll be given each piece as her journey unfolds. On the opposite side of the same coin, the Divine Masculine has all of the puzzle pieces and knows approximately where they go, but he can't yet see the full picture being formed. When the two counterparts work together in harmony, first from the inner union of their own masculine and feminine energies and then in physical relationship, they guide and support each other, each partner contributing to the union and the greater vision.

The Divine Feminine holds the blueprint of the journey and leads the connection through her healing and growth. Because she's the energetic connection, she typically experiences her ascension first. The Divine Masculine then guides the connection by navigating their journey in the physical world. This is typically infuriating to the Divine Feminine's ego as it often looks like she's "doing all the work," but the Divine Masculine is playing his role by being the energetic safe space for her ascension.

In the very beginning of my journey, I was massively triggered by a movie my counterpart and I were watching. Unable to hold it in any longer, I retreated into the kitchen where I had a full breakdown—snot-filled sobbing and all. My counterpart stood behind me in a sort of protective pose, comforting me as I processed the heavy emotions. I didn't understand until much later that this was a physical example of the Divine Masculine holding space within a sacred container for the Divine Feminine to transmute the energy and heal what had been triggered.

Once the Divine Feminine completes her healing process and moves into the next phase of embodiment, the Divine Masculine is initiated to his journey. The Divine Feminine has now integrated her inner masculine and feminine energies and is able to hold the space within herself and her connection, helping her counterpart transmute from that higher frequency. While it might take the Divine Feminine several years for her process, the Divine Masculine's ascension is both amplified and accelerated.

The initial lack of consciousness challenges the connection and is where the push-pull dynamic comes into play. To the human experience, this can be extremely painful for the Divine Feminine as her counterpart ghosts, rejects, friend-zones, becomes involved in multiple relationships, or engages in other triggering scenarios. Meanwhile, the Divine Feminine intuitively feels the strength of the connection, and this juxtaposition of her intuition versus what she's physically perceiving causes confusion and unrest in the dynamic.

The Divine Masculine is unconsciously playing out old patterns, perhaps even projecting his personal trauma and pain onto the connection, which triggers the Divine Feminine to have healthier boundaries, heal her abandonment or rejection wounds, or stand up for and express herself—all lessons she learns as she releases the distorted feminine aspect and rises into the Divine Feminine embodiment. Yet, the Divine Masculine feels just as much pain by acting from these distorted templates. The Divine Masculine loves his counterpart so much, the last thing he desires is to hurt her, and his soul only longs to be close to her in a healed state. He doesn't know why he acts or speaks as he does, but he's doing what he's designed to do—activating the Divine Feminine to become the best and highest version of herself, which prompts his own healing journey.

Now, let's again be clear that while we can understand the energetic workings of this journey, it's not to excuse or engage in hurtful behaviors. We're in no way about to invalidate the pain that can be felt from these situations and the very real emotional responses that stem from the human experience. This is where healthy boundaries, disengagement, or expressing yourself becomes a necessary part of your healing. However, as we ascend, we learn to see the soul, not just the human. Considering the connection from this higher perspective is a valuable piece of your journey's unfolding.

As the Divine Feminine reaches her inner union, it activates the Divine Masculine to begin his ascension. The feminine, now in the process of embodying her higher-self and standing in her light, triggers the masculine to rise—as the feminine aspect shifts, the masculine naturally shifts as well.

Let's use an example. Jill is a core Divine Feminine whose counterpart is Jack, a core Divine Masculine. As Jill energetically transforms and feels more empowered throughout her ascension, she's rising into her Divine Feminine essence, and by respecting, loving, and connecting to herself, she heals her inner masculine. Her inner masculine anchors in, now able to hold the full expression of her authentic nature with presence, stability, and security.

Meanwhile, Jack—physically seeing Jill in her empowerment or feeling the rise in her energy—or both—is activated to his ascension. He, too, is healing his inner feminine by understanding and trusting his intuition versus leading with just his logical mind. As his feminine energy heals, his inner masculine starts to rise. He recognizes and honors the feminine energy within himself *and* his physical Divine Feminine counterpart. This calls him to step up in his own life with a more stable foundation, taking responsibility with purpose and direction. He embodies the Divine Masculine essence. It's here that he takes the lead in commitment and connection.

The doorway to physical union opens.

REUNION & RECONCILIATION

We know by now that what we experience in our physical world is first experienced energetically within. "As within, so without" is a common expression outlining this spiritual law, but this goes for sacred union, too. As you continue your ascension, you create an internal shift that balances the polarized energies of your inner masculine and feminine aspects. As part of this process, you begin to experience greater harmony in physical form with your counterpart. I call this part of the journey the healing journey, otherwise known as the Twin Flame Journey.

Let's take another look at our diagram from Chapter One.

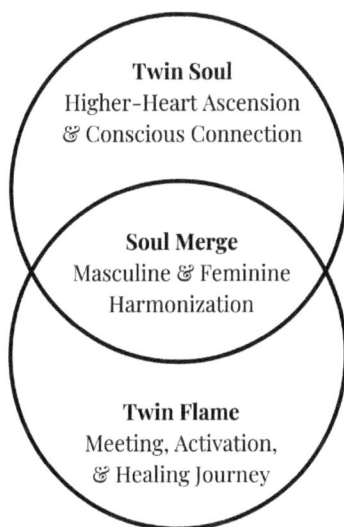

Twin Soul
Higher-Heart Ascension
& Conscious Connection

Soul Merge
Masculine & Feminine
Harmonization

Twin Flame
Meeting, Activation,
& Healing Journey

Once you reach the end of a significant phase of your healing and inner union journey, which can take months, years, or decades and can go through many cycles depending on your personal path, you'll start to enter physical union with your counterpart. Remember, this is an evolution, not a race. The ego favors urgency because faster means better in our society of competition and convenience, but as one of my favorite musicians, Trevor Hall, sings, "You can't rush your healing…" Your journey is a spiritual evolution, and it's perfectly designed for you.

While you've experienced your Twin Flame ascension with your counterpart—physically or energetically—it was still an individual process of healing, growth, and inner union. This next phase, what I call Higher-Heart Ascension or the Twin Soul Journey, is one of personal embodiment and conscious connection within a sacred relationship.

I like to differentiate between Twin Flame and Twin Soul in these stages because, again, even though they're merely labels, the term Twin Flame is energetically laden with romantic ideals, fear and pain, and even judgment of what the journey is truly about. For our purposes in this chapter, we're attaching special meaning to help explain the phases of this energetic experience. The Twin Flame stage feels heavy and dense as you're breaking away from the preconceived notions and processing unconscious wounds while the Twin Soul stage is peaceful, embodied, and connected. However, Twin Flame/Twin Soul both refer to the sacred, spiritual relationship in the beautiful journey home to yourself, God, and your beloved.

As you embrace your inner union, you not only intellectually understand that separation is an illusion, but you integrate this knowing within your personal embodiment. You're always connected to your counterpart, your union is within you, and your masculine or feminine is, always has been, and always will be part of you. Within this embodiment, you anchor more into your sovereignty and empowerment, release attachment to people, identities, experiences, and outcomes, and have faith and acceptance in the unfolding of your life. This intersection of faith and acceptance is your point of surrender, and it's in this surrender you secure your sacred connection to God.

In this next phase of your Higher-Heart Ascension, you'll still heal and grow, you might still be triggered, and you might still face obstacles and challenges along the way; however, you're doing so from a conscious place with healthy tools and resources now at your disposal. You're transmuting the triggered energy within a matter of minutes—or at the very least, much more quickly and easily—and you're peacefully trusting that no matter what's experienced in your physical world, it brings opportunity for guidance and growth.

Ascension doesn't mean everything is love and light and nothing "bad" ever happens, and it's definitely not about sweeping anything under the proverbial rug. Ascension brings the unconscious to light to be transmuted while recognizing that you *are* the light that transmutes.

This is your self-mastery.

Beware The Spiritual Ego

Before we continue, we have to talk about something that's pretty pervasive in the spiritual community: the spiritual ego.

The spiritual community spends a lot of time referring to "killing the ego" and "being in fifth-dimensional consciousness" and using the phrase "love and light" as its tagline—and I get it. Love and light is a beautiful blessing, and I even use the phrase as a send-off for all my channelings. But do we ever stop to think about what that means or how we're embodying that for ourselves?

Spirituality isn't a fad or a phase of life—it's a way of life, and a deeply personal one at that. It doesn't look or act a certain way, and it certainly doesn't adhere to click-bait quotes and sensationalized trends. Spirituality is substance. It's depth. And it's authentic to you.

Love to collect crystals? Me too! Into yoga? What a great way to stay fit and connect with your sacred breath. Like to swear like a sailor or speak poetically? Your choice of language is simply self-expression. Your favorite clothes are a pair of gorgeous boots or environmentally-conscious clothing? Rock your look! Craving scrumptious food with some sweet-tooth indulgence or maybe a raw food diet is more your thing? Chow down!

Spirituality isn't the words you regurgitate. It's the song your own soul sings. Spirituality isn't being beholden to proper language and grammar. It's expressing yourself authentically.

Spirituality isn't the clothes you wear. It's how you choose to present yourself to the world.

Spirituality isn't the food you eat. It's the mindfulness for how you feed your body while still appreciating and enjoying the pleasures this abundant life has to offer.

Spirituality isn't how many spiritual guides or ascended masters you connect with (though it's beautiful for you to recognize how connected you are!), or how many healing modalities you've learned (though it's incredible to have so many tools at your disposal!), or the number of tarot decks you own (though it's a great way to begin to hone your intuition and gifts!).

Spirituality isn't judgment and ostracism but acceptance and inclusion, and anything less is spiritual ego masquerading as spiritual enlightenment.

The spiritual ego is tricky, and the path of awakening is itself a journey of dismantling the false identity and what you believe spirituality to be. In the initial stage of awakening, you begin to see there's life beyond the daily existence of the routine you've been living. Then comes advocacy—the desire for things to be better, to change the world as you speak out on topics that inspire and drive you forward to create that change. We see this in the present global collective as "woke" culture—in protests and boycotts and individuals speaking out using their social media platforms. It's pretty incredible to see.

This rolls into a new level of awakening, which often lends itself to spiritual ego if integration is avoided or the energies are ungrounded. The next level of awakening requires you to examine previously-held beliefs, patterns, and views of yourself and the world, which can lead to a Dark Night of the Soul where faith is challenged and everything you've ever understood about yourself and the world is internally questioned. The problem is that most of the collective remains in the comfort zone of their previous knowing, creating cognitive dissonance, or resistance, when challenged to shift these tightly-held beliefs. We see this, particularly, in the deconstruction of fundamental religion.

But what is a belief? And where do those thoughts and perceptions come from? Are they actually yours, or do they stem from programming created within social systems you might not even be aware of?

At our earliest age, beliefs form from our experiences with family, friends, caretakers, and religious or education systems. Then, those foundations are built upon through higher education, work environments, entertainment, consumerism, and experiences with the justice system, medical system, legal system, and more.

Systems. Ways of doing things established by how they've been done before, forming collective beliefs, perceptions, and, on the more extreme side of the spectrum, judgments.

What happens if we take a closer look at our beliefs and where they originated? What happens if we dare to truly look at ourselves in our light and our shadows? What if we challenged ourselves to see through a new lens, an ulterior perspective? What happens when we begin to free ourselves from the shackles of society's perception and learn to stand in our truth, our authenticity, and our sovereignty? What if we take a pause when listening to authority, even spiritual authority, and trust in our innate wisdom and connection to self and GodSource?

The walls of "society" start crumbling down. For the first time, we begin to see the wizard behind the curtain for who he really is and ourselves for all we really are. As Frank L. Baum writes in *The Wizard of Oz*, "You've always had the power, my dear. You just had to see it for yourself."

This is the hallmark of spiritual awakening.

The honorable desire to change the world, along with the profound shifts taking place within, can lead to an elevated sense of self or superiority that gives way to the spiritual ego. Spiritual ego is an understanding of spiritual concepts and practices at great depth while still looking externally for resolutions or change; it's blindly following others rather than looking inwardly at oneself. It's the persistence of division and separation while speaking about unity and oneness—an "us versus them" mentality, exemplified in the popular phrase, "people are sheep." This continues to create division under the illusion of oneness while true unity consciousness understands there is no black and white, no right or left, but rather a middle way in which we all strive to exist. Everyone is on their own journeys, on a path perfectly designed for them while playing a beautiful part in the collective whole.

We'll all experience spiritual ego at some point in our journey— it's exciting to recognize our gifts, lift the veil, and become open to the whole of the Universe!—but this is the stage at which many can become trapped in a consciousness loop. Consciousness loops can display themselves in a number of different ways, including:

+ proclaiming spiritual authority or superiority;
+ judgment of others;
+ blame or projection on the external world versus self-accountability;
+ living from spiritual concepts and ideas (the mind) versus experience and embodiment;
+ repeating the same beliefs without room for growth or expansion;
+ living in a "good vibes only" mentality while shaming or judging your or others' humanity.
+ Even continuous healings, meditations, tarot readings, and energy clearings can create a consciousness loop!

Breaking free from the spiritual ego opens the door to your personal ascension, which is the final stage of spiritual awakening; however, even within the ascension journey, there are boundless levels and layers. To free yourself from the spiritual ego is to dive deep within—to the very soul of who you believe you are and the aspect of God you know yourself to be. It's not about looking outside at the world but inside at yourself that creates this shift—your higher-heart's truth, your connection to yourself and the Universe in its shadow and its light. It's a humbling experience in which you understand you are everything and nothing; you are all and none all at once. This is the integrated, conscious understanding that all ideas, concepts, and truths co-exist at once. Ascension is then the embodiment of this connection to yourself as one with the Universe and all contained therein, without exception.

Spirituality means acknowledging our human existence and remembering the authentic soul residing within physical form. It means seeing the darkness and giving it space and respect because even in the darkness, we grow. We can have doubts. We can be afraid. But through it all, we discover the courage, the strength, and the faith to walk through that darkness, knowing we are never alone and that we come out the other side transformed.

At its core, spirituality is about developing the connection between yourself and the Universe, bridging the gaps that create division between all aspects of yourself and another. It's about shifting your consciousness not to bypass the physical world but to become one with it, embracing your humanity as the expanding soul. It's about releasing attachment to labels and persons and things—all the self-identifying creations that make us think, as a trick of the ego, that this is all we are until we free ourselves and integrate the ego, until soul speaks louder.

Your ascension is the grounded integration of your higher-self in recognition of this sacredness within you and all. As you do your inner work of clearing old templates, beliefs, and patterns of fear, limitation, and lack, you're shifting your energy into higher states of being and connection to your authentic soul self. This embodiment—this authenticity—is leadership by example and is a testament to true spirituality. Through your capacity for love, compassion, and grace, you help others recognize this within themselves as they find their personalized spiritual path.

This is how we hold space for the global collective within the higher-consciousness energy of unity rather than the old template of division. This is what creates a shift in our personal world, and, through the ripple effect, this is what changes the collective.

Spirituality isn't what you do but who you are. You are unity consciousness.

HIGHER-HEART ASCENSION

Your Higher-Heart Ascension is the embodiment of your new state of being. It's the phase of your journey wherein you ground your spiritual nature into your physical experience, returning to your humanness but with elevated awareness and higher consciousness. This embodiment is the balance—the bridge—of everything you've learned and all you've so far become.

This balance is a necessary component of any spiritual journey. Ungrounded spirituality in one extreme produces spiritual ego, which can also lead to spiritual psychosis (this is different from spiritual awakening in that there's an eroded sense of physical reality and unawareness of the self, combined with fearful and erratic beliefs, mindsets, or behaviors). On the other extreme, too much focus on the physical world can disconnect you from your spiritual self, similar to your state of consciousness pre-awakening.

A shift in consciousness is permanent, though it might sometimes feel like you've regressed to old patterns and behaviors. It's like leveling up in a video game—you always return to the last "save point," but it might take some effort to find your footing again and "tune back in." This is why balance is key, and embodiment is the next step of your evolution.

What is embodiment, exactly? Put simply, it's the physical representation or expression of something—in this case, your spiritual essence. Until a certain point in your life, you were operating from a specific set of beliefs, patterns, mindsets, habits, and so on. Through your healing journey, you grow, expand, and evolve. You *become*. You're naturally standing in your self-empowerment, moving through the world with greater inner strength and fearlessly expressing yourself in your authenticity. You're no longer dishonoring yourself, no longer living in the core wounds of self-betrayal, self-neglect, or self-abandoning. You're living your values, living your truth, living your self-expression, and living your connection and your faith.

You're living in your divinity.

In this stage of your ascension, the feminine aspect is surrendered and trusting in the supportive role of the Universe by honoring her inner guidance rather than being led by the external, while the masculine aspect is acting upon that inner guidance with purpose and direction. You're claiming yourself and your place in the world, no longer afraid of hiding your light no matter how brightly you shine, and stepping into your self-empowerment and personal authority in everyday situations.

I want to add a quick reminder that this journey isn't about perfection, and this phase, too, is a process of integration where it will feel more natural the more you put it into practice. Have patience and compassion with yourself as you become more comfortable with this new version of you!

Inner union feels like peace, and that peace stems from within. The soul longs to know itself in its wholeness as one with the Universe. Coming into that sacred union within the self occurs when you begin to release templates of separation keeping you from recognizing you're already one with the Universe and always have been. While intellectually, you might already know this, as you embark on your journey of ascension—specifically the higher-heart phase—you begin to experience the *feeling*, the anchoring in. You might be more in tune with the energies around you and recognize your intuitive gifts as a more organic experience. Manifestations may take little effort without a need to practice visioning techniques because now you're naturally aligned with your soul's core essence.

This is your embodiment, and this embodiment has a ripple effect on your life experience. As you're personifying the energy of unconditional love and freely offering that love in your truest, authentic sense, that love returns to you tenfold because you're an open vessel able to give and receive in equal harmony. This is the masculine and feminine dynamic put into motion.

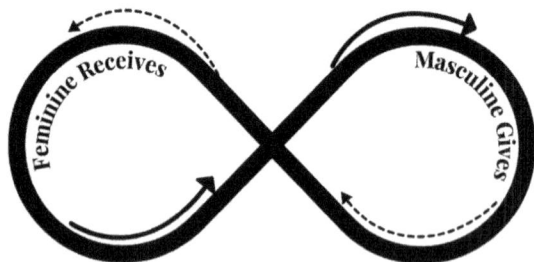

The masculine is the giver, and the feminine is the receiver. In union, this balance flows in beautiful, infinite harmony. You experience this within yourself as alignment and see it reflected in experiences easily manifesting in your external world.

This is the lesson the Universe is trying to teach us: be the love, be the magic. Let that flow through you without expectations of how or where that love is received by others or how or if it will be returned. Love knows where to go, and your role is to simply be the conduit to express love in the world. Once you accept this and live the energy of love, that energy floods into your life in every moment, every instance, in everything.

Love is the Universe wanting to return home to you. As soon as you recognize yourself as love, you recognize your oneness with all of the Universe.

This is unity consciousness.

Your sacred connection will naturally reflect this, as there's no longer a resistance or battle between the two energies. At least, as you go through this next phase of ascension, there will be greater harmony.

Reunion within the Higher-Heart Ascension will be unique to your personal journey. For some, the Twin Soul, as I like to differentiate it from the trigger-happy healing phase, will be the same physical person as the Twin Flame who activated you to your journey. This individual has been experiencing their own ascension and transformation right along with you—physically or energetically—and continues to be energetically compatible as you begin this next cycle.

For others, you may experience someone new who steps into the counterpart role to match your new energetic frequency and reflect your soul growth. This can happen for a couple of reasons: the partner that was labeled the Twin Flame could have been a catalyst partner to launch you on your sacred union path of ascension, and while they carried the energy of the Twin Flame, they may have been more of a soulmate or karmic connection instead. Another possibility is that the original counterpart known as your Twin Flame may be, through their free will, resisting their ascension, or they still have their karma to clear before coming into union.

Because you're meant to grow and manifest in your highest timeline, you might find yourself detaching from this original counterpart and calling in a Higher-Level Soulmate who matches your frequency and reflects this new level of ascension so you can continue to embody the highest energy of love. This person can be a life partner or remain in your life for as long as you both consciously wish. Your life is yours to create, and this is why releasing the attachment to the label of Twin Flame is so important—so that you're not fixated on a specific outcome and thus potentially delaying your personal growth. We'll talk more about the Soulmate Path in Chapter Seven.

Twin Flame Is An Energy

Everything is energy materializing into tangible form on this physical plane of existence. When you're created as a soul, you're birthed from the Mother-Father Source, similar to a child birthed from a biological mother and father. To conceptualize this, picture GodSource as a massive ball of brilliant energy giving birth to a little ball of that same energy shooting off into the Universe. This is you, as a soul, sent out into the vast Universe—like a child going off to school to learn, expand, and grow in consciousness.

Sometimes, that soul splits into two. This split isn't a separation, though our human minds have trouble perceiving it as anything else, but rather an expansion of that universal energy. The closest example might be in biology, wherein an embryo splits to become identical twins who share 100 percent of the same

DNA. On a soul level, you and your counterpart are the exact same "DNA" frequency.

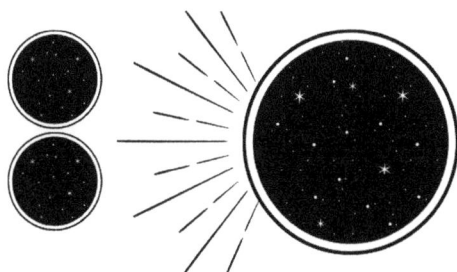

You then explore the Universe through different lifetimes and incarnations—even in other galaxies—learning and expanding for your soul's evolution, which, in turn, helps the Universe to expand. Eventually, you'll sense a longing to return as one in what's known as the soul merge or union.

Twin Flame is an energy that not only manifests within the physical vessel of your counterpart but moves through your world as a reflection of each other. Along your journey, you might experience the energy of your Twin Flame counterpart in another person wherein a friend, family member, or even a stranger might say or do something as only your counterpart would. In the beginning, it might catch you a little off-guard!

For example, one of my longest friendships is with a tried and true soulmate who, ironically, happens to share the same first name as my counterpart. During one of our catch-up calls, he said something I'd never heard him say before—a catchphrase my counterpart would often use. I paused, wondering if I'd heard correctly, and asked him to repeat himself. He did, then admitted he didn't know why he said it. I understood later it was the Twin Flame energy moving through my friend as a reminder of my counterpart's love for me.

The Twin Flame energy persists beyond the physical embodiment of your person. It's the unconditional love that exists within everything, including the God Source from which we come. This is why, when we talk about releasing the attachment to a specific person, it's not because that person isn't your counterpart—your ascension is creating shifts in levels of consciousness. The soul wants to evolve, and if, through unconscious choices, one counterpart is stagnating in their evolution by repeating karma and resisting human experiences, the Twin Flame energy may move through someone else so you can continue your journey in those new levels of consciousness.

One of our community members summarized our teachings perfectly when they said, "Twin Flame is an energy of pure Source love, the energy of the one soul, and if you have evolved through your healing to embody the higher-self, you can draw to you a different body with the same energy essence of love that is at your same level."

We're all experiencing a collective ascension where the bonds of co-dependency, control, manipulation, and other distortions no longer rule relationships. Sacred partners are at the forefront of the paradigm shift, creating heart-to-heart connections and writing a new template of divine love.

CHAPTER FOUR
SURRENDERING TO SEPARATION

"The reason why the world lacks unity, and lies broken in heaps,
is because man is disunited from himself."
– Ralph Waldo Emerson

IN ORDER TO FULLY UNDERSTAND union, we have to understand separation. It's the ultimate duality we're transcending—the core wound we all, as humans incarnated on Earth, experience until we remember that separation is and always has been an illusion.

Separation shows up in various ways in our lives. We'll experience separation as a loss—for example, the physical passing of a family member or friend—or as a change in location, such as moving or going away to school. We might even experience a sense of separation from a sport, practice, or hobby we once loved. Separation is anything that makes us *feel* physically or energetically apart from something or someone, particularly something that's deeply cared about.

Ultimately, separation is where we feel disconnected from ourselves, from love, and from God. We experience this first within ourselves before reflecting it onto our physical circumstances. When we're missing someone, for example, and we're feeling a lack of them, that feeling occurs within our emotional bodies. The more we tune into our heartspace and the energy underlying the situation versus looking at the situation itself as physical evidence for our pain, the more we can connect back to ourselves and remember that love, which is the essence of absolutely everything, always exists.

In the summer of 2020, I lost my best friend and soulmate of fourteen years—my dog, Riley. When I walked the halls of our local animal shelter as a volunteer in my early twenties, I almost passed his kennel on my way to take care of another dog. Something called me back to him, and together, we headed to the outdoor enclosure, where he grabbed a fallen stick and immediately began to play.

"You're all riled up!" I exclaimed joyfully to him, and some inner knowing sparked in my heart. "Your name is Riley, and you're coming home with me."

We experienced everything together. Riley was by my side every day as I fought my battle with Lyme disease, and he was my constant companion through the ups and downs of falling in love. He was there for every moment in between—my saving grace and greatest blessing. If you know the love of an animal, especially a soulmate in four-legged form, you know the absolute devotion you have to each other that words will never be able to articulate.

I've lost family members and friends, I've felt heartbreak and tragedy, and I've experienced life being turned upside down again and again. As much as I tried to brace myself over the years, nothing could have prepared me for this inevitable loss. Riley's passing was as peaceful as possible, but my heart was shattered. I was comforted by his younger sister, Moxie, by my faith in God, and by my inner knowing of the eternal—between my own near-death experience with illness and my work as a psychic medium, I couldn't help but trust in this. But I missed his physical presence—his nails tapping on the hardwood floors, his loud, nasally snores as he slept on his bed beside me, his big brown, expressive eyes begging for a fallen treat while I cooked dinner, and the "ah-woo-woo-woo" of his beagle-basset bark. We can know, without a doubt, what comes after, but we can also miss what was. This is where, as humans, we have to allow ourselves the process of grief.

It's also where, through our ascension, we're reminded to come back to the heart.

During those first few weeks of Riley's physical absence, I dreamed and had clairvoyant visions of him still with me. In my grief over the following months, however, I began to develop a sense of separation that, if I didn't have the level of awareness I did, I could have perpetuated, prolonging my pain of losing him. But the grief gave way to love, and the love, I remembered, always remains.

Even now, as I write this passage many years later, I allowed a pocket of grief to escape and held space for it. I connected to my heart. I shared my love for him, and I felt his presence in his eternal love for me returned.

Going through our ascension doesn't mean denying being human. Sometimes the experiences are challenging, and sometimes, they're downright miserable and just plain suck. But the more we can hold the space for our humanity in the container of our spiritual essence, the more we become the bridge for the two.

When we experience the energy of separation, we're in conflict with our mind and our heart, our ego and our intuition. This is where we create further separation in our lives. In our interactions with others, for example, we might get defensive and reactive, or we might withdraw and pull away, initiating energetic discord and even a physical separation.

Let's say our fictional couple, Jack and Jill, are engaged in conversation. Jill has unintentionally said something that's triggered an old wound within Jack. Hurt, Jack pulls away from the conversation and shuts down his emotions as a learned method of self-protection. Through this reaction, he's disconnecting from his emotions and separating himself from Jill and the conversation.

Jill physically perceives a change in Jack's posture, his demeanor, and even his facial expressions, and she energetically senses the separation building between them. Jack is no longer present in the conversation, but without communicating why or self-regulating his emotions to connect back to himself, this separation now becomes its own source of conflict. In her unconscious state, Jill might behave defensively or even withdraw from the connection herself.

"Fine! Don't talk!" she shouts and stomps away. Now the separation isn't only energetic, but physical.

In relationship philosophy, there's what I like to call the Wheel of Harmony. Conflict creates disharmony, but from disharmony comes the chance for repair, and from repair we return to harmony again. The repair stage is the most important, as it's here we consciously choose to mend ruptures and bridge the divide created from the original conflict.

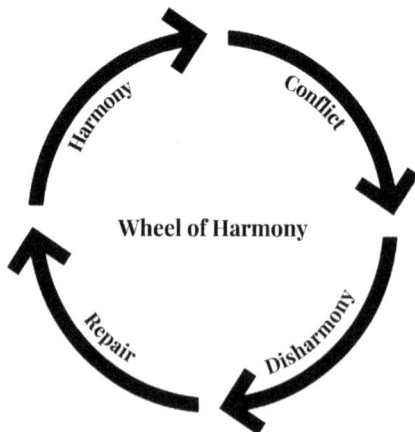

Wheel of Harmony

As everything is energy, we have an energetic relationship with everything. From people to money to jobs and anything in between, this cycle can play out in various life situations. For example, if you're struggling with finances, there's likely a conflict with money. This disconnection might stem from a feeling of scarcity or lack, and in order to repair it, you have to look closer at your money fears or beliefs. By clearing the energetic block— perhaps by starting with gratitude for the abundance you already have—you can easily return to a state of harmony. (For more on healing your relationship with money, check out our free channeling, *The Money Wound*.)

What if both Jack and Jill had approached this moment from a place of conscious connection? Aware of this disconnect within himself, Jack regulates his emotions and communicates his hurt to Jill right on the spot. This grants Jill the opportunity to apologize and approach the conversation with more love and compassion. Separation is transcended in honor of connection.

This is a simple example of how we can experience disconnection within ourselves, which creates further separation with others even when we long for closer connection. By bringing the unconscious to our awareness, it then becomes conscious. From that state of consciousness, new bridges can be built.

One caveat to this is the importance of honoring ourselves. Bridging separation doesn't mean we have to establish intimate relationships with absolutely everyone. In fact, always use your discernment when cultivating the connections in your life. Sometimes, it's appropriate to disengage, affirm healthy boundaries, or stand up for and express yourself. These are suitable responses that can keep you from disconnecting from yourself, especially where there are patterns of self-abandoning, self-sacrificing, or dishonoring. In this instance, you're disengaging from another's human or ego-self while still honoring their soul and your own.

Energies of lack, control, rejection, abandonment, unworthiness, and mistrust are all branches of fear that epitomize the core wound of separation. Those branches extend even further to other wounds such as insecurity, indecision, self-expression, jealousy, and on and on with each triggered experience.

But what is separation energy, really? We know it as a disconnection from ourselves and each other, but doesn't it go deeper than that? Yep.

Separation, as we know, is an illusion disconnecting us from God. But what we forget is GodSource is at the root of everything. Everlasting and eternally anchored, the roots are so firmly planted in the earth that we can't see them, but we have an innate knowing they're there. The more we heal these branches and connect back to the root, the more we transcend separation and realize that God is, and always has been, the whole of the tree itself.

LIFTING THE VEIL OF SEPARATION

As unconscious humans, prior to awakening and ascension, we operate on a lower-vibrational wavelength. This is where those dense energies of lack, rejection, and abandonment reside. When we tune higher and anchor into the divinity within ourselves, we begin to see how everything is interconnected. From this recognition, we release the illusion of separation and mirror back unity consciousness.

In our sacred channeling, "Out of the Garden," we shared the Garden of Eden as a metaphor for unity consciousness. The garden is abundant and prosperous, and within it, Adam and Eve are supported with everything they could ever want. No shame, guilt, or feelings of unworthiness are experienced there. They feel neither rejected nor abandoned. It's a veritable utopia.

The exiting of the garden is a fall in consciousness. Suddenly, Adam and Eve are shamed by their nakedness (humanity), suffer guilt for their choices (free will), and exist in lack and scarcity (separation). They feel abandoned and rejected by God, and they're plunged into a fear-based, lower-density energy. But what if they changed their perception of themselves and their experience? What if they recognized the divinity within their humanity and the ever-present support of GodSource in the gift of choice? What if they saw that the garden was still available, around them and within them?

What if they understood separation was only an illusion they were carrying as truth?

One of my favorite poets, Mary Oliver, wrote in her poem, *The World I Live In*, "I'll just tell you this:/only if there are angels in your head will you/ever, possibly, see one." The soul is deeply, intrinsically connected to the Universe itself. Through our ascension, we have the capability to break free from the illusions, to see through the lens of the higher heart, and to shift our consciousness to remember the limitless oneness of which we're all a part.

Let's go back to the Garden of Eden for a moment. Imagine Adam and Eve representing all of us as masculine or feminine energy, living in harmony and union with themselves, the world around them, and God. Again, there's no shame, guilt, or fear but love and unity. How can they understand love and unity without context, without knowing its antithesis? When you, as a soul, expand, the Universe expands, but how do you expand without understanding the contrast of contraction?

In Plato's *Allegory of the Cave,* a group of people have lived their whole lives facing a cave wall. They watch as shadows are projected onto the wall from objects passing before the fire behind them, the shadows becoming their only reality. This is akin to living in your comfort zone, not realizing that when you step out of that comfort zone, your world expands. Shadows aren't just shadows anymore, and there's more to experience than a simple blank wall. This allegory is a further metaphor for the Garden of Eden—as utopian as it might be, you're living from a limited perspective without understanding why it's utopian. You think you're living in paradise because you don't know what paradise isn't. In short, you're connected to God, but you don't know what it's like to not be connected to God.

This begs the question: How can we ever know unity if we never know separation?

Throughout our human experience, as particularly emphasized in fundamental religion, we tend to see God as something outside of ourselves. This is the collective fall in consciousness—it's the forgetting we experienced as we exited the proverbial garden, thus beginning our journey back home to the remembrance that separation is an illusion, and while we might *feel* separate from GodSource, we've always been connected.

This is your Higher-Heart Ascension. It's the deepening understanding that life isn't black or white, left or right, red or blue, either/or. It's both, and it's all. It's the middle way—the path between the two. It's you, as the physical example of this unifying energy.

In the TV fantasy-comedy, *The Good Place,* four humans are brought to what they mistakenly believe is "The Good Place," or Heaven in the afterlife, and begin a journey to become better versions of themselves. Through creative plot twists and character development, they end up in the actual Good Place, where they meet the famous Ancient Egyptian philosopher, mathematician, and astronomer Hypatia of Alexandria. Chidi, who was a professor of Moral Philosophy during his time on Earth, is thrilled to meet one of his idols, but when Hypatia casually forgets simple math and reduces her afterlife existence to drinking stardust milkshakes in her eternal state of happiness, the group begins to realize that even The Good Place has its drawbacks. With all desires met and in a state of constant perfection, there's no evolution or motivation for growth.

In Hypatia's example, she stopped experiencing and so stopped expanding. No longer using her mind, it turned to mush (as she calls it). This was unsatisfying for those in the group who had spent the series evolving through their experiences to become better people. Even in The Good Place, they yearned for something more. This led to the creation of a loophole in which they could decide to remain in The Good Place or return to the oneness beyond it. As one of the key characters says of his decision, "It wasn't like I heard a bell ring or anything. I just suddenly had this calm feeling, like the air inside my lungs was the same as the air outside my body. It was peaceful."

Through our ascension journey, we're becoming the physical embodiment of this choice as a bridge between the spiritual and human form by bringing Heaven to Earth. We're remembering the garden as part of us and the peace, the unity, and the oneness held within.

But before we remember, we have to forget. Sometimes we have to experience the darkness to understand the light.

Adam and Eve were known for being expelled from the garden, but if all is God and God is all, were they really cast out? Were they really separated from God and the garden itself? Or did they just feed into the illusion of separation as a fall in consciousness for us, in this space and time of mass spiritual awakening, to remember what our connection to God and each other really means.

When we feel separate and disconnected, it's because we've forgotten our divinity—that God is, always has been, and always will be part of us. When we feel lost, rejected, abandoned, or neglected, we're really only "playing out," as part of our human experience, our perceived separation until we heal this core wound by shifting our consciousness and recognizing that it's only a belief we've continued to feed.

We're all unique threads in the tapestry of creation—individual expressions of the whole. We've stepped out of the garden to experience this disconnect and remember there is and never has been separation. Eden—our connection to God—is always within us, and wherever we go, we carry that connection with us in the garden of the heart.

TWIN FLAMES & SEPARATION

You and your Twin Flame are one soul—that same singular, unique thread in the Universe's tapestry. You came to Earth for the purpose of your soul's evolution, playing all roles before incarnating in this present time as two physical vessels for your rapid expansion and to assist in the global awakening of the planet.

Meeting your Twin Flame activates lifetimes of energetic memory. The feeling of familiarity, home, and unity with each other is the soul's same recognition of love as when you were created. The pain of rejection, neglect, and abandonment is the soul's remembrance of when you were separated across lifetimes—or even within this lifetime—as well as the separation from God and yourself, all being interconnected. Add to this any of your own karma or experiences within your human existence, and you've got a hearty dose of projection you're unconsciously playing out with each other.

Imagine again Adam and Eve representing the Divine Masculine and Divine Feminine in a Twin Flame partnership. In the garden, you remember your oneness, your connection, your love. As you leave the garden and experience the fall in consciousness, playing out lifetimes of karmic cycles and unconscious roles, you forget your connection, you forget where you come from, and you forget yourselves as one. You might have lifetimes together in which you recognize each other as the beloved, but the pain of the original separation persists in the cellular memory.

Until now.

In this time and space of global ascension, you're clearing the illusion of separation, remembering your divinity, and returning to oneness with each other. When you reunite, the soul sparks in recognition of this oneness and love. Kundalini activates, and your chakras merge. Soul fragments are called back, and you begin to release all the soul sludge—all the unconscious patterns, programming, and beliefs keeping you in denser energy. You activate each other's healing and bring to the surface any pain or trauma housed within the unconscious and expressed in your human form. However, with the core separation wound still active, the love—and the light of that love itself—can feel too intense and overwhelming, and you begin to trigger these shadowed aspects of each other.

RELEASING TOXIC CONNECTIONS

I want to pause here and insert a disclaimer for Twin Flames and other sacred connections. Sacred partners will always carry an underlying energy of love, and while experiences within the journey may feel triggering and even toxic as individual traumas are triggered, there's never an excuse to continue to participate in a connection in which toxic behaviors are experienced—not even for your counterpart.

Sacred counterparts are not abusive. They may feel toxic or abusive when triggered, but they will never be intentionally cruel or deliberately repetitive in their behaviors. Triggered actions usually stem from a projection of old wounds and trauma that has nothing to do with your connection or each other. They're created from an unconscious response causing one to react out of familiar or learned toxic patterns. However, this is *no excuse* for mistreatment, and it's your responsibility to honor yourself first and respond with appropriate boundaries or disengagement.

Labels and fears of separation can keep us trapped in unhealthy connections, but this simply perpetuates unconscious wounds of self-abandonment, rejection, and even unworthiness. I'm speaking particularly of Twin Flames and sacred partners, but this also applies to any relationship or connection. Your first responsibility will always be to your care and well-being, including your mental and emotional health. You're not here to "fix" or heal anyone but yourself, and while you can support another person in their path towards healing, they have their own choices for their own journey. Unconditional love never equates to unconditional tolerance, especially when mutual respect is lacking. You can love the soul of a person without engaging in the ego.

I implore you to never hold onto unhealthy connections, especially ones that become toxic due to unhealed trauma and repeating patterns. Take time apart to heal the parts of you that might have once accepted the behavior. Where have you been toxic to yourself by allowing the behavior to continue? Where do you need to learn or implement healthy boundaries? Where have you been self-abandoning or neglectful of yourself, and where do you need to stand up and express yourself more? Every situation will reflect something about ourselves, but that doesn't mean putting ourselves in a holding pattern or remaining in the lion's den.

Time and distance can bring healing to the situation and, if it's a genuinely sacred relationship, to the connection. If you're struggling with toxicity in your connection, disengage to bring clarity to your mind and soul. You're *powerful*, not powerless, and certainly not helpless to this journey. Claim your power back by seeing where you've given it away.

When it comes to your sacred partnership, you and only you can know what the connection is to you, but that's not for you to rely on labels to keep yourself stuck in cycles where you're making yourself small. This journey is about expansion, and your true counterpart will always act as a catalyst and inspire you, energetically or otherwise, to grow.

Below is a quick exercise you can use to tune into the energy of your connection.

Harmonizing The Hologram

In your mind's eye, visualize a hologram of your person in front of you. Remove any projection, any memory of your experiences together, and any attachment to their name, persona, or physical identifying features so only their energy remains. Bring your awareness to your heart with a few deep breaths.

How does this person's energy feel? What sensations do you experience in your body? Is it restrictive or expansive? Is it harmonious or chaotic? Is there unconditional love or attachment? Do you feel safe, secure, and open?

Now, place your hologram next to your person. What do you see? What do you experience? Do the physical sensations in your body change in any way?

Be radically honest with yourself throughout this exercise. Your egoic mind might try to project the physical experience onto your holograms, but try the best you can to refrain for now. This exercise is about feeling into the truth of your connection through the higher heart versus the physical experience. It's teaching you to follow your peace.

Your soul's truth sees beyond the murky waters of the human experience. No one else can tell you whether or not your person is your counterpart, and no one can confirm for you what your connection is. This is a journey—your journey—guiding you back to your intuition and personal empowerment, and that means learning to discern and trust *your* inner guidance.

THE RUNNER-CHASER TEMPLATE

For most of our collective existence, humans lived in survival mode. It's part of the fabric of our evolution, a template passed down in our cellular memory through generations. The ego's gotten pretty good at protecting us as part of this survival mode—anticipating patterns and projecting fears all in an attempt to keep us safe—but as we're called to our spiritual awakening, we begin to realize there's another way of living: Soul Mode. The ego, unaccustomed to Soul Mode, activates its hidden programs of fear and doubt to keep us locked into the familiar, safe in what we know. It says, "Don't love too deeply—look what happened last time!" and "This can't be true—remember when…?"

In Soul Mode, we begin to listen without outside influence. We see with fresh eyes and a curious mind. We learn to follow our innate truth and keep our hearts open and available to possibility. We remember there are no limits, just a limiting world. We begin to understand the depths of ourselves.

When your real-world experiences seem counterintuitive to what your heart's telling you, your ego will launch right back into survival mode with old fears playing like a broken record. But these doubts along your journey serve a purpose. They offer the opportunity to explore places where the old template is still running and ask you to further your discernment skills to embrace your trust in yourself.

What does that mean for my physical connection, you might ask? *What do I do if my counterpart is ghosting, friend-zoning, or pushing me away?*

This head versus heart tug-of-war often results in a runner-chaser dynamic. The Divine Feminine, intuitively experiencing the sacred bond, will desire connection with her Divine Masculine because she sees the wider lens of the journey and can feel the energy exchange, even if it's not verbally expressed. However, the unhealed or distorted version of the Divine Feminine will move into more of a chaser energy (which can also look like or even activate an anxious attachment). The Divine Masculine, sensing the energetic pursuit from the Divine Feminine, will become overwhelmed by the pressure and try to pull away (which can also look like or even activate an avoidant attachment).

The Divine Masculine is the first to recognize or be attracted to the Divine Feminine—he might even initially pursue her—but this will generally be an unconscious experience. That is, he's not aware of the depth of feeling he has for her, nor does he fully understand the connection, but he feels a magnetic pull towards her with some of the same phenomena, intensity, and longing. Without an understanding of what this journey is, he'll try to apply logic to what is, in fact, illogical. As my own counterpart once said, "the heart is three steps ahead of the mind." The Divine Masculine doesn't necessarily understand what he's feeling or why, but his emotions are overwhelming as he's drawn to the Divine Feminine in ways he can't reason or explain.

Similar to the Divine Feminine before she understands the context of the journey, the Divine Masculine might try to compartmentalize or box the connection in with other experiences. Thinking it's the same as previous relationships, he'll deny or avoid the sacredness of the connection, even by avoiding or denying the connection itself. This isn't on purpose but comes from a lack of conscious awareness. This is part of his sacred union path of ascension in which he's called to align his mind (masculine energy) with his heart (feminine energy), especially where his emotional body and the feminine aspect were historically repressed.

The Divine Feminine, too, will unconsciously operate out of old patterns of control and manipulation until she surrenders to her journey. She might push for conversation, emotional intimacy, or recognition, which only seems to have the opposite effect. That push is actually her operating in her masculine energy in which she's trying to take action and lead the connection, which immediately repels the Divine Masculine, as this is ultimately his role. In this instance, the Divine Feminine is learning to surrender, to be in her receiving state, and to trust her intuition and the divine unfolding of her journey. She's being shown how to sit in the discomfort of her uncertainty as part of her dissolution of the ego, which likes certainty as it makes her feel safe and secure. But certainty is also an illusion, and safety and security are masculine traits she's learning to find within herself as part of her own energy versus seeking from the external masculine.

It's all a very layered journey, isn't it?

Let's go back to our favorite fictional couple, Jack and Jill. (In this example, as in all of our book, we're operating under the assumption that this is a true sacred relationship versus a toxic or incompatible connection. Part of your journey may be discerning between the two.) Jack, the Divine Masculine, and Jill, the Divine Feminine, experience a moment of discord when Jack pulls his energy back and stops communicating. This causes confusion and pain for Jill, who pushes for reconnection—perhaps she reaches out on all of Jack's social media platforms, bombards him with texts and calls, or even travels to see him in search of answers. Feeling insecure in her connection, Jill unconsciously attempts to manipulate or control contact as a means of security and validation.

Jack, meanwhile, isn't consciously aware of what he's doing or why. He doesn't *want* to disconnect from Jill, but he's overwhelmed by the intensity and flood of emotions he's suddenly experiencing. Because Jack doesn't yet know how to hold space for the complexities of his or Jill's emotions and thus doesn't have the energetic bandwidth to maintain the connection, he simply stops communicating. The more Jill pushes for connection, the more he finds himself withdrawing. He feels a sense of relief as he retreats, but there's a deep desire to be closer to her at the same time, causing his own pain and confusion. This is the push-pull dynamic mirrored in both counterparts.

You don't have to say it. I can hear the question now: *Why can't Jack just lean into the connection like they both want to?* (I may have worded this much more nicely than we've all thought at one point or another!) The thing to remember is so much is operating in the unconscious. Jack doesn't know why, nor does Jill, and this is where their healing journey takes root.

Jill's inner masculine energy might be repelling Jack's core masculine energy as she externally reaches for the safety, security, and validation she's meant to find within herself. Or, perhaps, she's being asked to step into her feminine energy of self-expression to communicate to Jack how his actions make her feel or to set boundaries around healthier communication. Perhaps she's learning how to surrender in honor of herself versus forcing the connection, trusting the communication to flow again when it's ready.

I know, I know. From the human perspective, it sounds like bullshit—Jill doesn't deserve to be treated this way, and why should she be doing all the work, anyway? If you're thinking this, then good! It means you're in an energy of honoring yourself first versus accepting poor (human) behavior from another. But remember what this journey is about. Your relationship is first an *energetic* connection in which you're both working together at the highest level to learn and grow. Don't forget that Jack's also experiencing inner healing within this spiritual partnership, even if it's not outwardly apparent.

On Jack's end, perhaps he's being guided to get more in touch with his inner feminine energy through understanding his emotions, or he might be discovering the value of being direct in his communication. Maybe he's learning how to regulate his nervous system so he can be present for Jill and her experience, which enables him to hold that container of energetic safety and security as the external masculine.

In this example, Jill's being asked to turn inwards and recognize her self-empowerment rather than seeking externally from her physical counterpart, which gives Jack room to regulate his emotional body and step into his core masculine aspect, magnetically drawing him closer as they build a healthier, interdependent connection with each other.

Looking within and healing the individual self doesn't invalidate both partner's need to show up for the relationship. Instead, it provides an opportunity for you to acknowledge and change unconscious patterns so you can *mutually* support and nurture the relationship in healthy and conscious ways.

The Divine Feminine is meant to experience her ascension first, and the Divine Masculine is playing a supporting role in leading her towards inner union—and a rather difficult role at that, as his soul wants to be united with the Divine Feminine just as much as she wants to be with him. At that core level, you are one—with your inner masculine and feminine energies reflecting in your outer physical vessels to show you where to heal, grow, and expand.

TWIN FLAMES: SHADOWS & LIGHT

On the highest level, the soul knows this triggering is meant to help each other clear any old energy that can't be carried with you as you evolve and expand. From the soul's perspective, you're acting in unconditional love to push each other's buttons and bring up anything that needs to be healed from the depths of your unconscious self.

From the human perspective, it can feel like shit.

Leonard Cohen once sang, "There is a crack, a crack in everything/ That's how the light gets in," reminiscent of the poet Rumi's wisdom, "The wound is the place where the light enters you."

Such is the nature of triggers.

You and your counterpart are the epitome of the yin-yang, with the black aspect representing the core feminine (yin) and the white aspect representing the core masculine (yang). Together, this image becomes the symbol for your union—two parts to one whole.

When the two "separate" pieces join together and lock into place, the wheel of destiny turns, becoming a metaphor for your sacred union path of ascension. But as we now know, you've never been separate at all. Within the feminine aspect resides the masculine, and within the masculine aspect resides the feminine. In this wholeness, you recognize and honor each other.

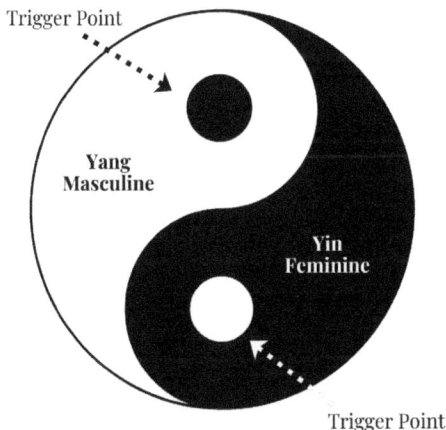

121

The feminine yin energy is the darkness—she's the depth, the wilderness, the caverns of the open heart. In her magnetic embodiment, she's mysterious, alluring, and quietly powerful. She's surrendered but not submissive, her energy flowing in the intuitive unfolding of every step. It's here that she shines. The white spot is the masculine light that's housed within her, asking her to burn brightly through the darkness from which she's emerged. This light is the trigger point for the Divine Masculine.

The masculine yang energy is the light—the natural essence of focus, direction, and leadership in his active masculine empowerment. He's the sun, which doesn't control in order to shine but is a fully-fledged force of power and presence. The black spot is the feminine depth that the Divine Masculine denies out of guilt, shame, unworthiness, and the repressed expression of his intuitive self, having found comfort in the caverns of his own guarded heart. This shadow is the trigger point for the Divine Feminine.

Trigger points represent the mirrored aspects of each other. The Divine Masculine is triggered by the light of the Divine Feminine, which only reflects his internal light that he can't yet accept within himself. The Divine Feminine is triggered by the shadow of the Divine Masculine, which only reflects her internal shadow until she integrates this into her wholeness. The trigger points are what you see when confronted with yourself—your very soul in another human form. Until you're ready to shift, you'll continue to reflect the trigger points in each other.

The Divine Feminine evolves through the darkness, and this evolution is the hallmark of a true Twin Flame or sacred relationship. In any other connection in which there are triggers and challenges, the feminine might make herself smaller, but this journey encourages expansion.

Ask yourself, are you…

+ making decisions
+ declaring what you want
+ taking action towards your goals
+ claiming space
+ being your authentic self
+ speaking your truth
+ sharing yourself
+ finding the power in vulnerability

Did you notice many of these contain masculine traits? That's because part of your expansion is recognizing your inner masculine energy in balance with your core feminine aspect.

The Divine Masculine pushes the Divine Feminine to grow more into her truth, her trust in her intuition, and her authentic self. She's forced to confront and heal her abandonment, attachment, and rejection wounds and embrace healthy boundaries and self-expression—and any other lesson encountered along the way. With his energetic support, he challenges her to rise into the full expression of who she is to become the Triple Goddess—a trinity archetype that manifests in the divine innocence of the Maiden, the nurturing creatrix of the Mother, and the infinite wisdom and maturity of the Crone in any given moment. The Divine Feminine holds the template of the Dark or Wild Feminine, as she's also known—fierce and formidable, yet full of mercy and grace. She is all things, and while the distorted masculine won't understand her complexity and depth, the Divine Masculine recognizes and honors her sacredness.

A meme once crossed my social media feed that read, "You threw dirt, and flowers grew. I'd be mad, too." This is the epitome of the Divine Feminine journey—the darkness is the depth, and in the depths of herself, she finds her light. In this blossoming embodiment of her personal empowerment, she shifts into her Higher-Heart Ascension of more harmony, peace, and unity. It's here she becomes an example for the Divine Masculine. It's here she leads energetically.

The Divine Feminine, through her growth, will unconsciously challenge the Divine Masculine to embrace his full potential and the embodiment of his higher-self to become the Sacred Warrior she knows him to be. In an act of mirroring, the Divine Masculine will do the same for the feminine in places where she kept herself small. The masculine energy is the natural giver while the feminine energy not only receives, she multiplies what she's given. The more the masculine pushes her to shine in her light, the more that light amplifies and reflects on the Divine Masculine in a bid for him to rise into his divine nature.

As you heal and evolve together, you reflect the shadow and the light, with these trigger points meant for the soul's expansion. Dark (the feminine lunar aspect) and light (the masculine solar aspect) create this expansion through the willingness to reach into the depths or "darkness" of the feminine energy to integrate the shadows so all becomes light.

TRIGGERING THE SEPARATION

When the energy system is overwhelmed and the triggers become too much, a physical separation will occur between counterparts as a form of divine protection. This is usually initiated by the Divine Masculine, who doesn't consciously know why he's acting the way he is, but when he's in tune with his emotions, he'll experience the pain of the separation just as much as the Divine Feminine. The Divine Feminine typically feels this separation as abandonment, rejection, or even simply the heartache of missing and longing for her masculine counterpart.

There were times in the beginning of my journey when I would leave my counterpart's house after a joyful day and burst into tears the further away from him I drove. I couldn't understand or make sense of it then, but it was the heart's yearning to be together and the ego's anguish of being "separated" again. In each instance, I had to let myself feel the emotions in order to release them and shift my energy to clear the illusion of separation.

Remember, true sacred partners will never intentionally hurt one another. You have an absolute love for each other, but it can be hard to remember this love when you're acting out of unconscious patterns, beliefs, and programs and bringing them to the forefront for healing. Because you don't *want* to keep hurting one another, separation ensues.

I once asked my counterpart if he ever thought of me when we were apart. My own abandonment wound had been activated, and I was feeling forgotten, wondering how we could go days or weeks without communicating if what we felt for each other was actually real. I'll never forget the way he turned to me, sincerity in his eyes and earnestness in his voice like he wanted me to understand, once and for all, the truth of his feelings.

"Every single day."

Triggers will continue until we heal the wounds, shift our perspectives, and remember that we're never actually separate at all.

I was once shown the metaphor of a boxing ring. Within the divine barriers of this boxing ring, you and your counterpart share love, communication, and joyful experiences. Then, you begin to trigger each other, giving or receiving little jabs from unconscious states of projection.

Let's use our go-to couple, Jack and Jill, as an example. Jack and Jill are in the ring, which, for the purpose of this metaphor, is their sacred relationship. Jack might find himself talking platonically to a female friend, which unconsciously triggers Jill's jealousy, insecurity, and fear of rejection stemming from a similar experience that occurred years before meeting Jack. Her pain body will be activated, and she'll react in the way that feels most safe to her ego—perhaps by withdrawing completely, or perhaps by taking a couple of jabs back. Jack, meanwhile, is completely unaware that this is a trigger for Jill or the reasons why, and he'll either push back or retreat from the connection for Jill to spend some time with herself and heal the energy that was causing her to project onto him.

This is akin to going to your separate corners. You're still in the ring together, but you're taking some time apart so you don't perpetuate the very cycles that you're trying to clear. Continuing as you were would only lead to a TKO and irrevocably damage the connection, but that's not what you're here for. You're here to heal and expand in love.

So, to your separate corners you go.

Now, I can't emphasize enough that this is all taking place unconsciously, and as you grow more aware of what's happening as it's happening, the more you can repair any disconnect in conscious ways together. Until that point, however, you might experience many rounds in your individual corners.

Healing The Triggers

Triggers themselves can occur in the most innocent of ways. For example, perhaps you and your counterpart decide to meet for coffee and one of you is late, triggering a fear of abandonment. Or perhaps the coffee cup is knocked over, spilling liquid everywhere, which triggers a fear of criticism or judgment. The circumstance itself is benign and may have nothing to do with the other person, but it's triggering something within you that's then projected on the situation. This is where the internal healing needs to happen.

If repair and reconnection aren't possible in the moment, usually because you're not operating in your conscious states, then separation may be healthy. It allows for space for both to reflect, claim personal accountability, and do the inner work necessary for reconnection.

Triggers are the places where you need to send more love to yourself. By triggering you, your counterpart is actually showing you where they love you, wanting you to recognize that love within yourself. Keep looking in the mirror to see what the trigger is reflecting.

The mirror won't always be a direct reflection. For example, if your counterpart is triggering you through their words, the mirror may not be the easy answer of "Where am I speaking negatively about myself" but, instead, "Where do I need to speak up for and express myself?" The mirror depends on the wound reflected, but in every instance, you're being asked to love and honor yourself more.

THE
CONSCIOUSNESS SHIFT

Before we embark on our ascension journey, we tend to act out of unconscious wounding, often projecting our pain onto our counterparts or other connections. We must have compassion for this unconscious version of ourselves—we don't know what we don't know. However, once we become aware of the pattern, it's our responsibility to shift to a healthier way of being.

The Divine Feminine, more conscious of this journey and what it entails, will actively begin her ascension first while the Divine Masculine energetically holds the space for her as she heals, clears, and shifts—though on the physical plane, this might look like separation or triggers that call up to the surface any pain or old beliefs housed in her subconscious. In this stage, there's an overemphasis on the Divine Masculine counterpart—not only is the Divine Feminine experiencing all sorts of phenomena, including vividly feeling his energy or presence, but she's dreaming and constantly thinking about him no matter how much she tries not to. He's just so *there*—always in the back of her mind and as part of her heart, and nothing can seem to turn it off. She might try to figure out what's going on with him in the same way she's trying to understand this connection—maybe by getting tarot readings or meditating in search of answers. At some point, she begins her inner healing work, and the Divine Masculine becomes the dangling carrot as she realizes the more she heals, the more the connection seems to shift.

In physics, this is known as Quantum Entanglement: two subatomic particles are intricately linked to each other across space and time, and a change in one will induce a change in the other. Evolving studies show how people share the same kind of entanglement in relationships. This principle helps to scientifically explain the concept of Twin Flames and the notion that you're never truly separate from one another.

As the Divine Feminine continues her healing journey, she notices incredible transformations in her connection with her counterpart and her own soul growth. She'll experience periods of absolute joy and euphoria to counter the healing of grief and anxiety, which might appear as extreme mood swings until the energies ground and settle into a more consistent state of inner peace. She'll have upgrades in her psychic and intuitive gifts and heart expansions that open her up to forgiveness and grace as more love takes root within her. Her physical world might also change as a result, and she'll begin a spiritual practice, focus on her health, revisit a forgotten passion, move locations, start a new job in a field of interest, and/or call in soul family to support her journey. If she began her journey in severe misalignment, this might look as if her world is turning upside down to make room for the new.

I like the metaphor of a house that's ready for an upgrade: you can't move the new furniture in until you clear the old furniture and clutter out—or, in this case, all the heavy, dense energy that might have served a purpose once as one version of yourself but that no longer fits the version you're becoming. The process depends on how much "clutter" you have, but the further along you go, the easier it becomes.

On an energetic level, the Divine Feminine's frequency is rising and her consciousness is shifting. As a reflection of that consciousness, her physical world naturally shifts with her. Everything is vibration, and only that which is tuned into the same vibration will be able to remain as part of a person's life, much like the frequencies of sound and a radio—only those tuned into the same station can hear the song that's playing.

The Divine Feminine will actively begin healing in several different ways, including journaling, guided mediations, energy clearings, past-life regressions, soul growth exercises, and other modalities she's called to. This might even be part of her own discovered spiritual practice, such as tarot, which also helps her tune into her higher-self and intuition. She might find herself crying in an emotional purge as repressed emotions are released through her physical body, or she might experience a physical purge with flu-like symptoms known as an Ascension Flu. (Remember to always consult with your physician on any physical symptoms you're experiencing.) This purge is the release of old energy connected to pain and trauma. The old always has to be released before the new can come in.

In occult teachings, the spiral symbolizes the journey of the soul, representing the soul's path from lower consciousness to enlightenment. On the ascension journey, the spiral indicates our inner growth—the deeper we go, the more there is to discover as part of our eternal evolution and soul recognition. There are many levels to this part of the journey for the Divine Feminine as healing, too, is an inner journey similar to an onion—the more you peel back the layers, the more there is to be revealed. For example, you might have thought you healed the rejection wound, but it will continue to show up as you dive further into memories, experiences, beliefs, or patterns as layers upon layers are cleared.

Imagine the wall of an old house that's been painted and repainted over the decades with various shades of color that other people chose. Your healing journey isn't about simply painting over the wall again to hide those old colors but scraping away each layer to unearth the original. That original color is you! It's your authentic soul self, and this is your new starting point. Now, whenever you want a new paint color, it's chosen with intention, and it's chosen by you.

There comes a point when the Divine Feminine starts to naturally integrate, anchor in, and embody this new (original) energy to such a point it's hard to remember she was ever anything but her authentic self. She becomes less concerned with the Divine Masculine's journey—what's he doing, how's he feeling, what's he healing—and becomes focused on the transformation occurring within herself and in her own life. She might even feel detached from her counterpart, and it's such a stark difference from the constant thoughts and intense energy from earlier in her journey that it seems like she's in a void. This void is the bridge to union, clearing any unhealthy attachment formed from the illusion of separation.

If you're stuck in a loop where you're constantly thinking about or analyzing the actions or words of your counterpart, consider first how this makes you feel. Where you feel helpless or powerless is where you're asked to surrender, as it's here you can make new choices and change the patterns. However, by continuing to focus on your counterpart, you're getting yourself caught in a consciousness trap I call the Twin Flame Matrix.

Where are you continuing to take responsibility for your counterpart's role in the connection or for the masculine's part of the journey? Where are you neglecting yourself or abandoning yourself by not choosing yourself, instead wanting to be chosen? Where are you not loving yourself as the Divine Feminine energy you are—one that's worthy of receiving love versus sacrificing or chasing for it? This is what your Twin Flame is trying to show you. They're always guiding your way home to yourself, but there comes a point along your journey where you realize you've held the map all along.

If you're struggling with these questions, return to the Distorted Masculine and Feminine Traits chart from Chapter Two and see where you can continue to clear these energies. Your counterpart is highlighting the blind spots in your healing; they're showing you where to mend the holes with more love. It's a reminder that you're always working together, even if it seems to the old paradigm of the physical world that you're not.

This part of the journey, what I call the transitionary stage, occurs in cycles as you continue to release attachment while anchoring into unconditional love. You begin to pull the focus off your counterpart and back onto yourself—nurturing your joys, supporting your passions, and developing spiritually rich connections. This instantly changes your vibration and shifts your frequency so you feel more empowered, more sovereign. At some point, you realize this journey was never about your counterpart but your return home to yourself.

This is the completion of one phase of your journey as you ready yourself for your Higher-Heart Ascension. Now, you're honoring yourself and embodying your highest frequency. You're integrating everything you've experienced as a lesson and a resource for your soul's transformation, and you're utilizing this internal evolution to expand your physical reality. You're shining brightly in your authentic truth and showing up in your external world, creating from a place of empowerment and abundance versus limiting beliefs and lack. Adjustments might be made as little triggers show up, but they affirm your inner work and anchor you more into your true self. Your masculine and feminine energies are creating union within.

THE POLARITY SWITCH

Once the Divine Feminine reaches a specific frequency in which she's embodying a higher state of honoring and expressing herself without the repeating wounds of the past, there's an energetic switch for the Divine Masculine to begin his ascension. Because the Divine Feminine leads the way energetically and naturally helps to transmute for the Divine Masculine, the Divine Masculine experiences his ascension rapidly. That is, it might take several years for the Divine Feminine to complete this phase of her journey, but because she's been clearing and healing for the two of them through her own evolution (remember: quantum entanglement), the Divine Masculine will ascend much more quickly. Still, the Divine Masculine has his journey to experience, and his healing isn't something meant for the Divine Feminine to take on.

The Divine Masculine clears his karma and shifts in consciousness through a much more physical process than the Divine Feminine. She operates more in the energetic realm and completes the majority of her ascension through healing work. The Divine Masculine, operating more in the material realm, completes the majority of his ascension through his physical experiences, including career or family circumstances, financial or legal situations, or relationships. It's here he begins to heal his inner feminine energy by opening up to his spiritual nature, following his intuition, and aligning his mind and heart. The Divine Feminine then experiences this switch by connecting with and grounding her inner masculine energy—shifting from a spiritual focus back to more physical enterprises such as her career, relationships, travel, and hobbies.

To the unconscious Divine Feminine, the Divine Masculine's ascension might look easier on the surface, but remember, not all is what it seems. His journey is essentially a trial by fire, and because he's not aware of the journey like the Divine Feminine is, it can be even more disorienting.

THIRD-PARTY ENERGIES

Third-party energies, as they're commonly known, are simply karmic cycles, experiences, or relationships that may present themselves along your ascension journey. They're referred to as third-party energies because, when considering Twin Flames, they seem to the human mind a type of interference preventing union; however, this is a belief that can keep you stuck in loops of powerlessness along the way. The more you shift your perception around third-party energies and see them for what they are—neutral situations or connections with which you or your partner are learning and healing—the more peaceful your journey will become.

You and your counterpart can potentially create your own cycle of karma through your mirrored projections, especially if you've experienced the majority of your journey physically together. This might give your journey the added challenge of releasing the past and healing any karmic patterns formed between you so your connection can move forward in conscious ways.

During your journey, kernels of doubt about your connection might crop up. Again, this doubt is there for you to look within your intuition for answers, not to find validation through others. You might research more logical reasons for your connection, such as trauma bonds, narcissistic/empath relationships, and attachment theory, and these can be extremely helpful in continuing to identify and heal the physical experience of your spiritual journey. For example, if you have an anxious or avoidant attachment or if you've experienced trauma bonds in the past, you might reflect on how that could be playing out within your Twin Flame relationship. Once that's cleared, however, clarity is received and more truth is revealed. In these sacred partnerships, what's left is unconditional love for each other and the intuitive understanding of your spiritual connection.

This journey teaches you to see with the heart versus your human eyes, even when your physical experience seems counterintuitive or even impossible. This is where you surrender, accept what's being experienced physically, and hold the space by focusing on your personal journey and self-empowerment. You're not putting your life on hold, but you're not blocking yourself from the connection or guarding yourself against love, either. It's a delicate balance that takes practice and patience.

When I was first activated to the ascension journey with my divine counterpart, it was in the middle of a difficult personal experience that could have seen us parting ways even before we came together. He called me one night a few weeks after our coffee date and openly expressed the circumstances in his life. I listened with compassion, appreciating the vulnerability in his sharing. This was a turning point, I realized. I had a choice. Did I want to continue with him and see where this led, or did I want to go our separate ways? I remember calling a friend who asked me simply, "Is it worth it?" A sense of peace washed over me like I'd never felt before, and every part of my being seemed to resound with a loving *yes*. Miracles unfolded, and we ended up growing closer than ever.

For many, third-party energies can look like circumstances or situations, like I experienced, or family, religion, culture, addictions, or marriage and other relationships. Usually, it's the Divine Masculine playing out these third-party, karmic situations and it's for the Divine Feminine to learn surrender, release control, and trust her journey. Beneath the surface of what it seems, all is for the benefit of your soul's evolution.

Wait, hold up, I can hear you saying. *How can that be?*

I know, I know… I'm not negating how awful it can feel to our human selves, and I can't tell you how many times I lashed out at the Universe or cried at the seeming unfairness and frustration of it all. But after we release that built-up energy and have our egoic meltdowns, which is really all they are, we have to look from the broader viewpoint of the soul's perspective versus the human mind.

Every experience is here for us to learn and grow—every single one, in a thousand different ways. However, it's hard for us to see this when we're in the thick of it. In fact, we might not understand the reasons for an experience for many months or even years afterwards, depending on how self-aware and in tune with our soul's growth we are. But they're there. Finding the lessons in the journey never undermines the experiences themselves as we remember many concepts, ideas, and happenings can coexist.

Part of the difficulty of the Twin Flame Journey, particularly, is learning to surrender and accept what's being shown. For example, if your counterpart is married, it's important to respect their relationship as part of their path. It doesn't mean your connection to them doesn't exist—this is where you have to continue your inner work to use discernment and trust your intuition—but just because you identify as a Twin Flame with someone, it doesn't mean you should uproot their life, or yours. Release the control and focus on *your* path for your soul's growth and evolution, allowing your counterpart the opportunity and space to do the same.

Karmic relationships, especially within the Twin Flame community, seem to have a negative reputation. Yes, absolutely, some people have toxic tendencies—there will be those who behave within the distorted templates of manipulation and control and who can be seen in a more hostile light. But remember when we spoke about karmic connections at the beginning of this book? We shared how important it is to look at these connections from an energetic perspective. Karmic connections are simply misaligned frequencies, playing out their soul contracts and thus healing within the relationship. Once karma is complete and the energy clears, the relationship naturally resolves. In the meantime, these connections serve the purpose of your counterpart's—and yours—evolution and growth. Whether or not your counterpart is learning and growing from the connection is up to them.

It's also up to you, energetically speaking. If you're focusing on your growth and transformation, then your counterpart, due to that quantum entanglement theory we talked about, will naturally reciprocate this in their journey, too. However, if you're leaking your energy by putting too much emphasis on your counterpart and their karmic relationship, it's another way in which you're chasing (and thus pushing away) your own connection. You're disempowering yourself by looking outside of yourself rather than fueling the connection from within.

In simple terms, if you're focusing so much outside of yourself on another's connection, you're helping to create this as part of your reality. By releasing the concern for the physical experience—particularly one over which you're not a part and have no control—you shift the energy back to yourself, which creates a shift in the energy within yourself.

In the very beginning of my journey, I found myself feeling insecure of my counterpart's connection with his ex—or, more accurately, the bond they shared as parents to their beautiful little girl. Even though they were no longer together, I thought there was no way I could be as close to my counterpart as his ex was, and I tried pulling back from my connection with him time and time again. I was always afraid to interfere, feeling like an outsider, wondering how I could ever have a place in his life—wondering how I could ever compare. Sure, I'd birthed businesses and books and creative ideas, and sure, I'd been a caretaker for others practically my whole life, and sure, I was a mom to my beloved dogs, but I wasn't a mother in the way it seemed to matter. I didn't even know if I wanted to be a mother, and the trauma I experienced with illness made me think I'd never become one. It triggered my insecurity, my fear of non-acceptance, and my own self-criticisms and feelings of unworthiness. As I did my inner healing around this—and with his insistence that he wanted me in his life—I quickly began to shift my perception and experience gratitude for his ex. I saw her as a beautiful soul who helped bring his daughter into the world—a little girl I love with every fiber of my being, who I'm deeply connected to, and who I consider my soul daughter.

Throughout our journey, I held the vision of harmonious co-parenting and helped him raise their daughter. I became good friends with his ex, who refers to me as their daughter's bonus mom and frequently expresses her gratitude for me, too. Interestingly, she would often remark that while she's more of a masculine mom, their daughter needs my feminine energy around her, and I always deeply appreciated this and respected her place as their daughter's biological mother. Having the chance to love his daughter as a family and be part of her life is one of the greatest honors and blessings I will ever have.

I could have easily let my insecurities get the better of me, but I didn't want that for anyone. I quickly learned that my counterpart's connection with his ex didn't negate my connection with him or the beautiful connection I had with his daughter, and over the years, we bonded together as an extended soul family.

This is the ripple effect you have on the world around you. As you heal, connections and dynamics have a chance to heal with you. Karmic partners and soulmates may be able to teach you and show you what your counterpart can't—at least, not while you're continuing to play out unconscious patterns. If you were to engage in some of these experiences with your counterpart within the unconscious state, you would simply be passing the mirror back and forth, ping-ponging the projection onto each other and creating more damage to your energy fields.

Instead, on the one hand, your counterpart will learn through the experience of third-party relationships or situations to liberate you from the pain and projection. On the other hand, you'll be asked to deepen your inner work through any triggers that come up, which will create huge, abundant transformations in both your lives.

CHAPTER FIVE
UNVEILING THE SHADOW

"Someone I loved once gave me/a box full of darkness./It took
me years to understand/that this, too, was a gift."
— Mary Oliver, *The Uses of Sorrow*

DURING OUR SPIRITUAL ASCENSION, WE'RE called to awaken to
a deeper level of conscious awareness, seeing beyond the illusory
veil of the physical world we once identified with to understand
the sacred essence of our soul. Part of that challenge comes from
moving past the lower-consciousness realm of duality.

Shadow work is the internal self-study of repressed or hidden
aspects we may have previously rejected or judged as "dark" or
"bad" in this dualistic landscape. The more we recognize these
aspects and draw them to the surface, integrating both the
light and dark, positive and negative, the better we're able to
connect with the wholeness of who we are, heal our subconscious
projection on others, and live with full authentic and conscious
awareness of self.

The shadow-self was coined by psychiatrist Carl Jung to represent repressed personality traits we keep hidden from ourselves
or others. Usually created in childhood through trauma or other
painful experiences, the shadow-self includes the light and dark
attributes we don't particularly like or accept, pushed deep into
the recesses of our subconscious mind. These shadows can then

appear without our awareness in our everyday experiences as repeating habits, patterned interactions, and mirrored projections in others.

By moving beyond self-judgment and befriending our shadow with compassionate care, we can take an honest look at what this shows us about ourselves and how we live our conscious lives. It's here we have the opportunity to heal and create from a new place of awareness.

INTEGRATING THE SHADOW

Shadow work is an often-intense healing process that makes the unconscious conscious. It's a tool that helps us shift patterns and beliefs to live with greater wholeness of the self, leading to deeper levels of inner peace and love. The more you bring the shadow to your awareness, the more you can heal and clear its energy. Through your healing, you're choosing to break free from the unconscious influence the shadow holds over your life and embrace a new way of being.

I often refer to my experience with illness as an example because it was such a catalyst for my own inner healing. I'll be real—Lyme disease was the most suffering I've ever known. I wasn't only struggling with physical pain, but it also brought me into a mental and emotional darkness I couldn't have ever imagined. I felt trapped in my mind and betrayed by my body as my life was turned upside down by a damaging disease no one seemed to understand and even doctors ignored. Writing—this great love of my life—was my catharsis. I wrote blog posts, articles, speeches, and a book. I journaled my way through the pain, always finding my way back to hope by the end. Writing helped me understand my feelings so I could begin to move beyond them.

When I was activated to my ascension journey, I delved even deeper into this healing. Trauma was still housed in my body and my belief system, but as I worked my way through the shadows, I found that I didn't have to wallow in the depths of that pain anymore. Now, when I connect with other Lyme patients and caregivers as part of my non-profit work, sharing my story to remind them they're never alone, I know I can sit in the darkness with them, but I don't have to stay there.

This is what healing does. It guides you out of the darkness, helps you transcend the haunting of your pain, and brings the shadows to light.

Shadow work is a practice that requires discipline and self-compassion, as facing yourself can be the hardest thing you'll ever have to do. However, like anything, the more you do it, the easier it becomes. Once the shadow is integrated, the energy of the past painful experiences becomes neutralized and no longer unconsciously rules your experience. Turn to your support system of trusted counselors, therapists, mentors, and friends as you move through this process. There's no reward system on the other end other than your own transformation, but as you transform yourself, your world changes, too, and this is a reward in and of itself. The more abundant you feel, the more abundant you become. The more you embrace your self-love, the more loving you are and the more you're open to receiving love. This is a natural law of the Universe.

Shadow work requires openness and vulnerability, but you, yourself, are the safe space with which to begin. Your awareness is the key as you look at what's being mirrored back to you through your interactions and experiences in your physical world. This isn't about taking the blame or responsibility for another's actions or behaviors or carrying the weight of shame and self-criticism. On the contrary, it's about empowering yourself through self-accountability. We can't control others' actions or even our external environment and experiences, but we can be mindful of ourselves.

The reflection is then an opportunity to ask yourself where have you contributed to the energy and how can you empower yourself to make more conscious choices? The more self-aware you are, the more successful you'll become at integrating the shadow.

SHADOW WORK EXERCISE #1 KEYS TO CONSCIOUSNESS

Your emotions are the key to understanding your experiences, and your physical body is the barometer for those emotions. If your body is tense and closed off, explore the reasons why. What are you feeling? What emotion is this stemming from, and what is that emotion trying to tell you? Once you understand your emotions, you can build awareness of the beliefs attached to them and begin to shift the pattern.

The Emotion Sensation Wheel, created by licensed therapist Lindsay Braman, is an excellent way to get in tune with your physical body and the emotions housed within. Like our Core Wounds Tree in Chapter Four, all physical sensations come from a feeling that boils down to a basic emotion. For example, maybe you're feeling tense, unsteady, or cold. These physical sensations could be an indication of an activated trauma response (fight, flight, freeze, or fawn), which is rooted in fear. On the flip side, maybe you're feeling calm, soft, and open—all physical sensations contributing to the basic feeling of happiness. Paying attention to your body can help you identify what you're feeling, which can then guide you to the core emotion and all that's associated with the experience.

In the Keys to Consciousness exercise, use the Emotion Sensation Wheel (available in any online search) to help identify keywords you might be feeling and journal about your experiences. What triggered that feeling? What was your reaction? What other emotions are associated with it? For example, if you've experienced a situation in your relationship in which you found yourself feeling jealous, write down the keyword *jealousy* and ask yourself what caused this sensation? What other feelings or emotions does this provoke? Irritation? Hurt? Insecurity? Now, what is the root emotion of that feeling and why? In this example, maybe it's a fear of rejection or abandonment. Continue to explore and dive deep into any beliefs or patterned experiences that might come up as a result, and don't be afraid of any emotional release during this process. Your emotions are an energetic purge that's part of the healing.

If you want to go even further with this work, you can add this next component to your journaling exercise.

Ho'oponopono

Ho'oponopono is a Hawaiian prayer of reconciliation and forgiveness that roughly translates to "make right" or "bring back into balance." This healing technique is based on the spiritual notion that everything is energy, and we have the ability to shift that energy, including our relationships with others, through healing ourselves.

While Ho'oponopono can be used in forgiveness for others, it's especially powerful when turned inwards to reflect on our contribution or role within a situation that may have caused strife or conflict. This promotes the Law of Responsibility, one of the karmic laws that says we must take responsibility for our thoughts, decisions, and actions. It's the conceptual idea that nothing happens to us, it happens for us—what are we going to do with the experience, and how are we going to learn and grow? Ho'oponopono is a powerful method of holding space for these thoughts, decisions, actions, and even feelings that may have resulted from or led to the wrongdoing. This leads to conscious self-healing, which also allows for healing with another.

By reciting the prayer or pairing it with more concentrated reflective practices, such as journaling, blocked energy is released for healing, enabling you to move forward with more love and a refreshed mindset. When spoken as a repeated mantra, this prayer also works as a powerful activator of self-love.

Ho'oponopono is a prayer in four parts. Speak all four parts out loud as a simple repeated mantra or consider the keyword of the trigger and journal each section in depth as a practice for greater self-awareness and clearing.

I'm Sorry

This part of the prayer asks for self-responsibility and the acceptance that everything that comes into your awareness and physical experience is part of your creation.

Please Forgive Me

In conjunction with the above section, ask for forgiveness for your contribution in the circumstances or the role your consciousness played in the creation. You can be as specific as the situation warrants.

Thank You

Find gratitude for the experience, the lessons, the growth, or the awareness. Allow yourself to thank the other person involved, GodSource, the Universe, or yourself. In this step, gratitude energetically frees you.

I Love You

Love is the most powerful force there is. End the prayer with love for yourself, GodSource, another, or for anything that feels like it needs love to return you to your natural state of peace.

For example, if you find yourself sacrificing yourself for others and resenting them for it, your trigger keyword might be *people-pleasing*. Your Ho'oponopono journaling might look something like this (allow yourself to go as deep as you'd like in reflection of your feelings):

> I'm sorry I made the decision to sacrifice myself for the needs of others in order to please them or gain their love. Please forgive me for seeking love outside of myself and not having firmer boundaries in which I can more healthily offer myself and others love. Thank you for showing me where I need to set and maintain healthier boundaries. I love you, I love God, I love myself.

SHADOW WORK
EXERCISE #2
THE MIRROR EFFECT

We know by now that our interactions with others, whether in intimate relationships or brief connections, are our greatest catalyst for growth. This is because people act as our mirrors, a reflection of ourselves. Twin Flames or sacred partners are our ultimate reflections because of the spiritual significance of the connection, and it's here we feel safe to explore the most vulnerable and intimate aspects of ourselves—even the aspects we don't necessarily want to see! This is the crux of our shadow work.

However, the mirror isn't always a direct reflection, such as "They're angry, so I must be angry." Rather, the mirror highlights the experience so you can explore your connection to yourself. If someone is angry, how do you feel about anger? What belief do you hold? How do you respond to it? Your conscious awareness will always be your superpower, as it's through this awareness you have the ability to shift any beliefs or patterns by remembering you're not those beliefs or patterns.

Begin this exercise by taking a piece of paper and drawing a line down the middle. Think of a person or a situation you might be struggling with. In the left column, write down every keyword you can about this experience (hint: use the Emotion Sensation Wheel as a guide), including pleasant or unpleasant thoughts and beliefs you might hold about this person or situation.

Let's say, in the height of conflict, your partner says something insensitive. In the left column, write down everything you can think of about your partner in a stream-of-consciousness style: loving, generous, thoughtless, inconsiderate, etc. Yes, some of your keywords might be contradictory but don't worry about that just yet, and try to refrain from any self-judgment. This is a brain dump of everything you're perceiving and feeling about your partner in this moment. Go even further by exploring the experience in your journal and see if any other keywords pop up. For example, how was your partner being insensitive, and how did it make you feel?

Now, spend some time with each keyword in the left column and in the right column ask yourself, is this true? Pay attention to the sensations in your body and your intuition as you explore this perception. The egoic mind creates beliefs based on past patterns and experiences, and it likes to make up stories to fill a narrative or justify an emotion. Place your hand on your heart to connect to the energy within and find the soul-truth.

If the answer is no, it's not true, then write down the truth. Your ego might begin to fire off in protest, trying to make it true, but keep working through the belief that's held until the ego is dismantled and the shadow is integrated. If the answer is yes, ask yourself why it's true and consider what you can shift within yourself when it comes to this dynamic. If your partner is being insensitive, do you need to disengage from the situation, set healthier boundaries, or express yourself more? Does this situation reflect your own insensitivity, or is your sensitivity a point to address within your connection? You might even want to return to this later and see if it still holds true at another time—what might be true in one instance might not necessarily be true as a whole.

What you're doing here is neutralizing the energy. When you hold an emotion, that emotion forms a belief. By bringing the emotion to your awareness, you're giving yourself the opportunity to explore your perception of the person or situation before the belief sets in. You can practice this exercise for everyone—even loved ones and positive experiences for a greater understanding and awareness of yourself as a reflection of the love you see in others.

Shadow work isn't just reconciling the more negative aspects of ourselves but also bringing to light the positive. Through this healing, you're meant to be loving yourself. Never forget to come back to the love within yourself, for yourself.

SHADOW WORK
EXERCISE #3
BECOMING THE MIRROR

Speaking of loving yourself...

In shadow work, it's sometimes easier to start with other people because of our everyday interactions that are nearly impossible to avoid. It's always harder to look at and face ourselves directly in our own mirror. This is particularly true when battling insecurity and a lack of self-worth, but remember you're not your insecurity, and you're not lacking in any way. These are merely beliefs instilled in you from your upbringing, life experiences, or even society itself.

Through your healing, you're completely reimagining and rewriting the script you've been playing out for most of your life—recognizing who you truly are, and who you want to be.

And guess what? This matters. You matter. Your internal transformation creates a ripple effect on your life and everyone around you. Through your healing, you're helping to facilitate healing for others because you, too, are a mirror. The more you remember you are love, the more you exude that love, and the more that love reflects onto others. Pretty cool how everything is interconnected, isn't it?

For this exercise, you'll need a hand-held mirror (if you don't have a mirror, you can use your cell phone). Look at yourself in the mirror for as long as possible, even if it's only for a few seconds at a time. Have patience, compassion, and kindness for yourself, and know your limits. This exercise might be a little more difficult because you're looking at yourself without the distraction or projection of others, but it's supposed to be a practice, not a punishment. As you gaze at your own reflection, you'll likely find yourself becoming uncomfortable—the mind will start to chatter, and you'll begin to notice little imperfections or insecurities.

This isn't you, yourself, that's speaking and noticing these things but the ego's memory that's being activated. It's the criticisms and judgments of others, including our collective society, that were embedded into your subconscious and that you internalized as true. These beliefs have continued as a shadow, keeping you from recognizing your authentic self for most of your life. Remember yourself as a child? How you looked in the mirror and loved yourself, how in your innocence you proclaimed your uniqueness or your beauty or your talent with such confidence? That's who you truly are—your inner child knows and remembers, and so can this version of you.

Looking in the mirror, begin repeating affirmations and notice how you feel. Start simply: *I am beautiful. I am valued. I am worthy.*

I am loved. Repeat these phrases, feeling into your heartspace, as powerful emotions are evoked. Explore these emotions with one of the other shadow work exercises as a supplement, but continue to affirm, without criticism or judgment, the essence of who you are. You're beginning to reclaim your power by honoring yourself and your place in the world. You're shedding the ghost of past influence and following the voice—and truth—of your soul.

SHADOW WORK EXERCISE #4 GREMLINS TO GIZMOS

This exercise is my absolute favorite and my personal secret weapon, and I'm sharing it with you because I know firsthand how putting it into practice can help you change your life.

Back in the early days of my spiritual awakening, I had a mentor and beloved friend who was guiding me through my grief over the loss of my grandmother. In one of our mediumship sessions, she brought forth the following affirmation to help ease the anxiety that had accompanied me most of my life: "All is well in my world."

Later, she taught me a visualization technique to enhance the affirmation and deflect the negative chatter that would unconsciously infiltrate my mind and create a downward, depressive spiral. Whenever you become consciously aware of a negative or intrusive thought, immediately imagine a stop sign in your mind. Hold it up in front of you, making it as large as you need it to be, and focus on it. Once you stop the unconscious spiral, you can then acknowledge where the thought came from and explore any emotions that come up as a result. This exercise isn't to avoid or repress negative thoughts but to cease their cyclical pattern.

I've said it before, and I'll say it a thousand times: your awareness is your superpower. The mind is such an incredible tool that, when aligned with your heart, it helps to create your personal reality. Your imagination shapes your very world, and your perceptions and beliefs then color those experiences within it. Think about it: if you're in a critical or judgmental state of mind, it dampens even the most pleasant experience; however, if you're in a joyful or peaceful state of mind, it feels like you're on top of the world! This is the power of your thoughts.

Visualizing a stop sign wasn't enough—at least, not in the long run. When I was activated to my ascension journey, I found I needed something more to not only pause the downward spiral but to change its direction entirely. I began to imagine those negative thoughts as gremlins turning back into Gizmo from the 1980s film *Gremlins*. You know the one… "Don't feed them after midnight!" Picturing the gremlins transforming into the sweet and cuddly Gizmo certainly made me feel better, but I wanted to prevent falling back into old patterns again—I wanted to raise my vibration and sustain that energy. So, I added a little flavor to my visual. Not only did the gremlins become Gizmo, but I imagined Gizmo farting hearts.

That's right. Farting hearts. Never imagined I'd be writing those words in a book, but here we are!

The thought made me laugh so much that it immediately shifted my energy, and I knew this would be the trick I needed on my journey to mindfulness. I don't use this visualization technique much anymore, as this practice has created a natural shift wherein I can now recognize the thoughts and transmute the energy almost immediately. But I still have the graphic I created of Gizmo farting hearts sitting on my desktop, and whenever I look at it, it makes me laugh and reminds me how far I've come.

I hope someday this exercise does the same for you.

CHAPTER SIX
HEALING FOR HAPPINESS

"Have enough courage to trust love one more time
and always one more time."
– Maya Angelou

OUR PHYSICAL REALITY IS THE hologram reflecting our inner Universe. If we truly want to make a change and create a new and better world for ourselves and generations to come, including nurturing healthier and more conscious connections, it starts with each individual doing the inner work—facing the shadows, healing the pain patterns, and transforming the old templates. It means diving deep to see where beliefs were formed and clearing the conditioning for us to become our true, authentic selves.

Sometimes this starts externally—with poets and preachers sharing their lived experiences and learned wisdom to initiate our personal truth and resonance. We read books and take courses and listen to podcasts or lectures that create a spark of recognition within us, and we learn to follow that spark as a compass for beginning to intrinsically understand who we are. But there's only so much we can learn externally...

The real journey is the one found within.

There comes a turning point in our lives when we direct our attention inwardly and follow the path of honoring our lived and learned experiences. We're driven to radical honesty and personal transparency, asked to excavate the deepest wounds to free ourselves. Light appears when we dare to witness our own profound truth, and that light is carried to the darkest shadows without shame or fear. It's here we're challenged to peel back old layers of who we thought we were and all we thought we believed to become who our soul knows us to be. It's in these moments of raw vulnerability and intimate connection, starting with ourselves, that we begin to change the course of our lives.

Wisdom is found in the healing and honoring of our sacred heart.

SACRED ANGER

We've learned through our ascension, as part of our shadow work, not to deny any aspect of ourselves, including the wide range of emotions we experience as human beings. We're asked to acknowledge and observe these emotions, bearing witness to them as guides for our journey. Yet, anger is one such emotion that often gets overlooked.

Anger, and its complementary threads of frustration and tension, can be a sacred energy if used properly and expressed in healthy ways. When anger is held for extended periods, it becomes poison—festering in our emotional bodies and harming our nervous system. This suppressed energy becomes a cocktail for distortions such as resentment, which breeds irritation, which leads to aggression, which can erupt in violence and abuse in its more reckless, unconscious expression.

Too often, anger is suppressed for fear of conflict. This is especially true for the feminine aspect where, in our current patriarchal society, confrontation is more often than not met with severely distorted masculine energy. Sacred anger becomes reactive anger, which creates disconnection and damage. However, when anger is expressed and received with honored intent, it becomes righteous and just and can move mountains.

As a Libra sun sign, I'm usually all about the peace, harmony, and goodwill towards all. I tend to choose my battles, both because I've never been comfortable with conflict due to my specific wounding and because I like to weigh the matter—how important is it in the long run, really? But I've also got an Aries moon that, with its passionate edge and aligned with a strong sense of justice, will kick some ass to ensure I'm holding firm to my boundaries and staying in my self-empowerment! It was my counterpart, a peaceable yet fiery energy himself, who taught me to acknowledge anger as having its place in our human experience.

"It's okay to get angry," he told me once during a heated discussion. "It makes you real."

He wasn't afraid of confrontation or the full spectrum of my emotions. As I expressed myself more fully in the raw authenticity of all I am, including moments of anger and frustration, he stayed. I'd never really let myself experience that before. He reflected to me where my distaste for conflict gave way to avoidance, and he challenged me to show up more for myself, as myself.

Like any emotion, anger holds value and has its place in our energetic toolbox when approached consciously and with healthy communication. It shows us the shadow, the resistance, and the blocks within ourselves by pointing out where we're holding ourselves back. When we get to the root of anger, we begin to acknowledge even deeper aspects of ourselves—where have we been betraying or abandoning ourselves? Where is it necessary to instill or uphold firmer boundaries? Where do we need to speak up or express ourselves?

Your voice is your greatest gift, and activating your sacred anger, particularly when you've been conditioned to silence yourself, is part of your soul's evolution in self-expression.

HOLDING SPACE

In J.M. Barrie's *Peter Pan*, the narrator explains, "Fairies have to be one thing or the other, because being so small they unfortunately have room for one feeling only at a time. They are, however, allowed to change, only it must be a complete change."

Being human, you have the capacity to hold space for more than one emotion—or energy—at a time. This expansion is the very crux of your ascension. You're not limited to one thought, one feeling, or one experience. You're a multidimensional soul continuing to evolve, and through your evolution, you're learning to embrace all possibilities.

The Divine Feminine experiences this expansion as part of her emotional body. Where she might have once felt overwhelmed by emotion, swinging wildly off-balance from one to another, she now can hold space for all through the masculine container of her inner union. For example, she can bear witness to her sacred anger while still connected to the energy of compassion. She can feel her heartbreak and observe her disappointment and still experience forgiveness and love. Everything can coexist at once and be held in the space of the heart.

This is a key component of unity consciousness.

The Divine Masculine's capacity to hold space for himself and his counterpart also increases as he continues to evolve. The masculine's previous relationships mirrored his existing levels of consciousness, which is why the connection to his counterpart initially feels so intense. All of a sudden, he's confronted with the complexity of the Divine Feminine. She embodies more love, more expression, more depth than he's experienced from relationships in the past, and his limited container is unable to hold such energy. However, as the Divine Feminine evolves through her ascension, she challenges the Divine Masculine to rise with her. His expanded relational container creates a foundation for their joined union.

DON'T FEAR THE VOID

Before a breakthrough to the next level of your journey, you might feel like you're being pulled back in a slingshot, tension and anticipation building as you wait to be released. You might feel jaded, cynical, or even burned out from all the inner work you've been doing. Maybe you feel disconnected where once you felt so connected, or maybe you're facing doubts and questioning everything.

This period of uncertainty is known as the void.

The void can feel scary when you don't know what's happening—or when it feels like absolutely nothing's happening!—but you can think of it like a cosmic cocoon where you're being asked to hold space for yourself. You might be called to rest more, or you might experience a cycle of non-productivity or lack of motivation. Sometimes your physical body simply needs a bit of a reprieve to recalibrate and catch up to all the internal changes. Even if you can't see it, so much is still moving energetically.

Surrender to the present moment and use this void to identify what might be triggering you in its discomfort. Go back to the basics of your journey with some energy clearing or inner child healing—nurture yourself with your favorite childhood pastimes like coloring or Legos or a beloved family movie to connect back to yourself. Allow yourself to receive what your soul is calling for and trust your intuition to guide your way.

This period isn't anything to fear, and it won't last forever. You might feel disconnected—like you've gone "offline"—but don't forget that separation is the illusion, and you're always connected to God. When God seems to go quiet, you're simply being asked to tune deeper into the heartspace as a call for surrender, to trust the process, and to listen more closely to your innate wisdom.

Try not to be too hard on yourself in the void, as it's a time of compassion and self-love. What would you say if you were speaking to your sacred partner? How would you treat them? Would you pressure them through this period, or would you hold space and encourage them to nurture themselves and seek support from their community or soul family? You're being called to hold this space in loving self-care as you prepare to shift into a new level of your journey.

Remember that you, yourself, are ever-expansive and full of infinite possibility and potential. As you progress in your ascension journey, you anchor into the higher-frequency embodiment of that possibility and potential with more joy, peace, and love in your life.

PEELING BACK THE LAYERS

The ascension journey is one of inner growth. Rather than a linear, once-and-done experience like our human minds might be used to, it's a healing process that happens in layers. Throughout your journey, you might experience residual energy resurfacing, making you think, "Hey, wait a minute. I've already cleared this!"

Layers.

I like to call the healing process an excavation because we're tunneling our way through lifetimes of old energy accumulated through our human experience—ancestral patterns and generational beliefs and societal programming—to rediscover the core essence of who we are as soul.

Let's consider the layers of the Earth as a fitting metaphor for our spiritual journey. First, we have the crust or the surface layer. The crust could be seen as spiritual awakening, as it's here we begin our journey and start to peer beneath the veil to recognize there's more than meets the eye. It's also here that some choose to remain and where surface spirituality such as "love and light" is maintained.

We move down through the superheated mantle—a pretty accurate example of our ascension activation! In this layer, we begin to burn away the false ego and any templates, programs, and parts of ourselves that might have served us at one point in our lives but that no longer hold true for the authentic soul we're just now meeting. This is the hard part—it's where our physical lives are dramatically altered as we end or shift fractured relationships, change jobs or careers, move locations, and even release habits and addictions. Inwardly, we're grieving past versions of ourselves and stepping into the new simultaneously. This is where the bulk of our shadow work is completed, and it's also here that we can find ourselves stagnating in our growth or getting caught in consciousness traps.

Next, we have the outer core, which is its own protective layer, and the inner core, which is appropriately named in our metaphor to represent the soul essence. The outer core might reflect our Higher-Heart Ascension, where we embody more of our authenticity within the new frequency of higher consciousness. It's here we might begin service work and anchor or evolve more into our soul's mission. We might welcome in new soul family or find ourselves shifting or mending established dynamics to more conscious connections. In this layer, we're called to embrace our inner union and enter into sacred relationship with our Twin Flame or divine partner.

As we excavate each layer, we're chipping away at what was once solid rock—deconstructing our fundamental beliefs and egoic identity. This releases dust and debris, or the residual energy of your former self that's being dislodged and brought to your awareness for further clearing. You can also think of this as your soul's initiation before you level up or break through to the next phase of your journey. Have you closed out all of those old cycles? Have you anchored into your faith, following your soul's guidance versus the ego patterns of the past? Have you allowed yourself to go deep enough to clear the core of any outdated beliefs?

The ego isn't meant to be killed or completely eradicated—it still serves a purpose for our human experience as part of our personality within this physical world. But we're *dismantling* the ego from its previous patterns and cycles to become more in tune with the presence of the integrated self. Ego no longer directs or controls our lives. Instead, we discover through the many layers of our ascension that our eternal soul was always meant to guide us.

SHADOWS TO LIGHT

You've done the deep dives. You've faced your fears, unlocked core beliefs, and rewrote the story of who you are. Amazing! You should be so proud of yourself for how far you've come in overcoming past aspects of who you used to be. But remember, shadow work isn't just excavating the darkest corners of yourself. Through the shadow, you're meant to recognize your light.

While we tend to focus our shadow work on taking accountability for our mistakes, healing trauma, and shifting patterns, the point of the ascension journey is to come home to our fiercely-loving selves. Forgiveness of your past mistakes helps you become a more compassionate person, healing your trauma helps you recognize your courage and strength while giving you a voice to stand in support of others, and shifting old patterns helps you learn to see yourself and the world from a wider perspective, inviting in new stories and experiences. Your shadow work grants you these gifts and more as part of honoring yourself.

Our human life is meant to be a joyful expression of our loving souls, but in this lower-density experience that our world has become, this has gotten somewhat lost in translation. This is where we're called to shift. Through your ascension, you're clearing away the heavy energies of lower consciousness and raising your frequency to hold *more*—more joy, more abundance, more pleasure, more peace, more love. You'll start to see this in your personal experiences as you change locations to new environments that feel like home, as you accept new jobs that ignite your passion *and* support you, or as you welcome conscious connections that grow through encouragement in reciprocated affection.

With every step, your soul is guiding you to the best and highest version of yourself within your physical vessel, and your life is meant to be an expression of that. It's not some outward goal to achieve or a far-off destination to reach. It's lived here, now, in every moment. Throughout lifetimes, including this one, you may have experienced suffering to learn the overcoming of it, but you're not meant to stay there.

You had to know the shadow to recognize the light.

DIVINE SURRENDER

You've completed your triggered ascension process, and now you're moving through dimensions of consciousness to anchor that higher-embodied energy into your heart. This isn't to say you won't experience challenges or struggles, but you know how to alchemize the triggers and shift the energies to stand in your self-mastery. You're reclaiming joy and love as part of your very essence as soul, and through your rebirth, you're releasing anything not aligned with this authentic expression.

This is your peace, and your peace is your power.

Power doesn't mean control and force, just like peace doesn't mean passivity and inaction, nor submission and silence. As you embody higher consciousness, you learn to take responsibility for yourself and your creations through your choices, operating from a place of sovereignty and personal authority. You learn to embrace your authentic self-expression in honor of your sacredness. You learn that peace is found in your connection to yourself and GodSource, and within that connection is a surrender that bridges faith, trust, and acceptance.

But what is surrender, really?

True surrender, like the kind we learn along our spiritual journey, is nothing like we know surrender to be through the warped lens of manipulation and control. True surrender isn't sacrificing the self as the martyr or conceding to one's will by playing the victim; it doesn't mean betraying yourself and abandoning your values. True surrender isn't submission to the external, material world—whether that's a person, collective, or experience—or relinquishing your personal authority. These are all distorted responses to power plays for dominance and the world's ego striving for control, which we've been conditioned to believe.

True surrender is divine surrender, and divine surrender means trusting your soul as one with God. Within the peace conceived from this surrender, you find your power.

THE TENETS OF SELF-LOVE

Self-love is frowned upon in a society that all but encourages the exhausted, overworked, and burned-out spirit. Nurturing and nourishing yourself is considered selfish, while sacrifice is considered noble. When you embark on the spiritual journey, you begin to understand the deception of such ideas and how they've permeated the very fabric of our culture. As the old saying goes, "You can't fill from an empty cup."

Ascension teaches us everything is balance as we learn to walk the middle way—honoring ourselves *and* each other or being able to give *and* receive. Self-love, as a component of self-care, not only helps you nurture a deeper communion with yourself but also with others, including your counterpart. Here are some ways you can continue to love yourself along your sacred union journey...

Self-Honoring

Self-honoring can also be known as self-pride or self-respect. In fact, they're all shades of the same energy of loving yourself. Honoring yourself presents itself in several different ways, including:

∞ Physical appearance: The popular phrase, "as within so without," doesn't just relate to our experienced reality but to ourselves as a whole, as how we present ourselves is often a reflection of how we're (consciously or otherwise) feeling within. Your physical appearance isn't for the benefit of others. Instead, the more you discover and claim your authentic self, the more deeply you connect to your self-expression by allowing your outside appearance to reflect the inside, including your emotional state. Want a boost of internal confidence? Wear that new dress that makes you feel beautiful! Seeking nurturing and comfort? Maybe it's a sweatpants and slippers kind of a day. Honor yourself by honoring your unique expression and emotional needs in every opportunity.

∞   Physical environment: As your external world is a reflection of your internal world, your physical environment becomes its own component of self-love. Ask yourself where are you the most physically, mentally, and emotionally at ease? Where do you feel spiritually connected? What helps you raise your vibrations and simply feel good? Whether it's immersing yourself in nature or cozying up in your favorite room, your surroundings influence your well-being, and being mindful of your physical environment is an effective way of honoring yourself as you begin to cultivate more self-love wherever you go. By tending to your inner sanctuary, you then transform any space into a sacred reflection of your inner peace.

∞   Healthy boundaries: One of my favorite quotes is from Stephen Chbosky's *The Perks of Being a Wallflower*, in which he writes, "We accept the love we think we deserve." Boundaries are another form of mutual respect, coinciding with how you value yourself and setting expectations for the way you want and deserve to be treated. Healthy boundaries create stability and security within yourself, which reflects in healthy connections with others. While the word itself might seem to be a form of separation, boundaries allow for the nurturing of more intimate relationships as you understand how to honor yourselves and each other.

Spiritual Rest

Rest is essential for those on the ascension journey, least of which because it refreshes the mind, body, and spirit, allowing you to become more focused and clear-intentioned. As powerful light codes stream onto the planet to assist with our collective ascension, you might feel the effects as a call to sleep more, turn inward, ground in nature, or simply sit in a state of being. There's so much occurring energetically that the physical body needs time to adjust and "catch up" to these new energies while higher levels of consciousness are integrated. You might even find yourself subconsciously releasing and clearing old energies or receiving new insights about your sacred partnership within an active dreamstate!

Rest is a type of spiritual recovery that can take many different forms: physical rest or sleep, emotional or mental rest, and creative rest. Tune into and listen to your body and what it needs. Don't force or push yourself too much, and make sure you properly nurture yourself using the other self-love tenets.

Intuitive Trust

One of the most important tenets of self-love is what I like to call Intuitive Trust. This is all about listening to your inner guidance and allowing yourself to trust what you're receiving. Trusting your intuition helps to guide everything from interactions to next-step actions to what you consume. If you're called to certain foods, for example, what is your body telling you about what it needs? Dense foods could be a call for more grounding. Favorite sweets could be inner-child nurturing. Consumption can also include entertainment wherein the more attuned you are to yourself, the more you'll find yourself guided to specific books, television shows, or movies that carry significance for your journey.

I truly believe everything comes into our awareness when we need it, and when we become conscious of the world and our connection to ourselves, we're able to put the pieces together and understand how the Universe (and our higher-self) is guiding us every step of the way. Some books will stay on my shelf, unread, for months until I'm guided to them, and they somehow speak to exactly what I need in that moment, or I'll reject watching a popular television show only to come across it years later and find meaning reflecting my current circumstances. This is even true for fresh viewings of old favorites! Watching *How I Met Your Mother* now, for example, is a different experience than it was over a decade ago for all I've since learned about conscious connections. Similarly, a second viewing of *The Good Place* affirms innate beliefs while adding layers to spiritual concepts. When I turn to my own novels, written at the height of illness and struggle, I recognize the stories were once my catharsis, leading me through intense emotional trauma. Now they're the story of personal revolution—my triumph in the overcoming.

Such is the beauty of art. There are a thousand interpretations, all relating to the present state of consciousness. Breakup songs become anthems of self-empowerment. Movies evoke their own philosophy for the life we'd like to lead. Books speak to the story of the soul as we journey into more of who we are. As we expand and evolve, the world around us does, too, and there's no greater evidence of this than in the art we're guided to experience and create—art that transcends time, planting seeds for trees we may never see grow.

Discernment is crucial when honing this intuition, as the ego and outside influences can easily pull us from our inner knowing and personal paths. Listen to your body for clues in any given situation, as your body's physical response will indicate whether or not you're following your intuition or your ego. Is your body excited or relaxed? Does the situation feel peaceful and "right"? That's your soul's guidance giving you the green light. Is your body feeling restrictive or anxious? Does the situation feel tense and somehow "off?" Give yourself permission to reconsider.

This discernment can be especially helpful when interacting with your Twin Flame or sacred partner.

"Life is messy," God said to me one day as I considered if an action I was guided to take was coming from my ego or my heart.

I'd spent nearly an hour driving around in circles, wondering if I would be perpetuating a cycle if I reached out to my counterpart like I was being called to, not wanting to resume the runner-chaser dynamic that seemed to haunt our connection, with me at the helm of the chasing. The fear-filled part of me wanted to just go home, but I couldn't seem to bring myself to steer in that direction. Even though we'd been in a period of prolonged separation and there was little logical reason to see him, my heart kept guiding me to his front door.

I chose to trust where I was being led, feeling unprepared but anchoring into faith. God's words were an echo in my soul as I mustered every ounce of courage. I later realized there was so much more at play than the simple act of a face-to-face conversation. For my part, I was healing my fear of confrontation, my fear of rejection, my fear of expressing myself authentically and without reservation. There were no planned speeches or fantasies or overthinking. I had to get over myself and let my soul guide me where it needed me to be. I had to learn to take some risks and live it all out loud.

Life is messy because we're human. But God granted us the gift of our intuition to help us navigate our humanity. Honor yourself by listening to and trusting your inner knowing. Only you know what's best for you and where you're being guided.

HEALING & HARMONY

In my ascension series, *Healing and Harmony*, we look at common core wounds and keywords to help you activate your healing and bring you into greater soul resonance. Feeling betrayed by your counterpart? Betrayal causes deep-seated disappointment that reflects grief or anger and emerges as general heartbreak. This disappointment stems from the inherently brave act of allowing yourself to become vulnerable enough to set reasonable expectations of trust with another. However, when that trust's broken, it creates a thread of wounding that asks you to look at the energy of betrayal from all perspectives, including taking accountability for the betrayal of self—in what ways did you abandon yourself or defy your intuition?

The answer to healing betrayal is never, "I just won't be vulnerable or trust anyone ever again! So there!" That's the foot-stomping, arms-crossed temper tantrum of the ego that perpetuates the pain by trying to protect itself. To heal means to shift, not shut down, and this begins with you. It means allowing yourself to get deeply intimate with your specific patterns and shed light on the shadow aspects that contributed to the experience. It means keeping your heart open and connected to the love within yourself.

Healing means shifting the energy to shift the experience.

This is an example of healing transforming into harmony, which is the crux of your sacred union path of ascension in partnership with another. Healing and harmony in sacred relationships always start with consciously connecting to the healing and harmony within yourself.

CHAPTER SEVEN
RETURNING TO LOVE

"Love is born into every human being; it calls back the halves of
our original nature together; it tries to make one out of two and
heal the wound of human nature."
– Plato, *The Symposium*

THE DIVINE MASCULINE SHOWS US how to be attentive and
aware of our thoughts within the beautiful power of the mind as
a creation tool. He teaches the Divine Feminine how to control
and observe her thoughts in the liberation of her authentic self.
Through the container of presence and security that he provides,
he creates space for her to balance the overflow of her emotions
and embrace her higher wisdom.

The Divine Feminine shows us how to trust the guidance
of the intuition in support of a higher vision. She teaches the
Divine Masculine to see beyond the intellect to the power of the
unguarded heart. Through her intuitive nature and openness, she
helps him acknowledge his inherent worth and grounded strength,
activating him to the full expression of his conscious self.

In partnership, you and your counterpart are always guides for
each other, elevating your ascension. Once this is honored, you're
able to work together in sacred connection to help each other grow,
create, and expand beyond any perceived limitation.

This is love in union.

One of my favorite depictions of the Divine Masculine and Divine Feminine union is seen in The Lovers card in *The Gilded Tarot* by Ciro Marchetti. In this card, a male wearing (what appears to be) Roman armor is lifting a female in supportive embrace. Her back is arched, chest open and expanded, as golden light pours down from the Universe into both their hearts. It's my favorite card in any tarot deck (ever) because it's the pure essence of the Twin Flame connection. Here, the Divine Feminine is the healer in her ability to receive the energy and pour into her counterpart while the Divine Masculine is the warrior, his strength uplifting and sustaining her.

This is the birth of their sacred union. In this union, they both embody the new healer-warrior template. Two parts of one whole, each brings their individual strengths and healing energy into balance. This is first seen in inner union—wholeness and harmony of the self—and then in conscious communion with each other.

As you heal the illusion of separation and move into the Higher-Heart Ascension, you'll experience the process of reunion and reconciliation with your counterpart and lay the groundwork for physical union. With some exceptions, perhaps, this happens as a process versus the grand declaration we've been conditioned to expect from Hollywood romances.

That's not to say you won't have these magical moments—the Universe is filled with magic, and you're meant to enjoy all the playful, loving experiences you desire! But romance is an energy— it's the love you have within yourself expressed as part of the world around you versus seeking something externally from your connection with another. Romance isn't only the flowers in bloom or the sunset walks or the starlit dances. It's the beauty and wonder and delight at this co-creation with the Universe and the love that's both expressed and received. While the sacred, intimate moments of courtship we usually affix to the romantic label are shared within relationship, romance itself is an extension of the energy of love.

Your journey is, first and foremost, one of expressing this love to yourself.

Ascension teaches you about true love—love without attachments, without conditions, without expectations. It shows you how to love with presence, have meaningful connections, and enjoy intimate experiences. We're called to transcend the old templates of what we were taught relationship to be and return to the Christ-Sophia consciousness of unity, oneness, and sacred love.

This is the sacred union. It's a marriage of opposites joined in an alchemical transformation of pure, divine Source energy. Experienced first as the *hieros gamos* soul merge within, the masculine and feminine principles expand, transmuting all lower-density energy, to embody higher-consciousness states of peace, harmony, and love in oneness with all.

In your empowerment, you're claiming your place in the world in harmony with others, no longer hiding or dimming yourself for the sake of expectation or fear of judgment but shining in your divine right. Competition ignites inspiration and motivation instead of scarcity and insecurity, and self-expression adds your unique imprint to the Universe's design. You're following the path of peace through your deepening connection to yourself and GodSource and mindfully challenging patterns and beliefs as they're brought to your point of awareness.

You're embodying your true essence as your authentic soul—more so now than you've ever done in any version of your life thus far.

Recognizing this union within, you realize you've always been in union; you've just been clearing away the cobwebs of illusion that conditioned you to believe otherwise. The more you embody this inner union, the more you see it reflected in your physical world, including your sacred relationship with your counterpart.

For some, you'll experience this next level of your sacred union path of ascension with the same counterpart with whom you've been activated to your journey, as, physically or energetically, you've been growing and transforming into higher states of conscious embodiment alongside each other. Your "second chance" will seem like you're meeting each other for the first time, all over again. It's an opportunity to start over without the unconscious projections and distorted patterns of the past. For this to be successful, however—and this will be a natural part of your ascension process—you have to be willing to forgive the past and get to know each other again as the new versions of self you've both become.

For others, you'll literally meet new counterparts or high-level soulmates who are at your level of consciousness, matching your shifted frequencies. Your "second chance" will be a fresh opportunity to embody higher levels of consciousness and an understanding of your ascension journey in connection with another. These ascension partners might be with you for a short time to reflect your growth and help you continue to expand in the highest energy of love and support, or you might choose each other as life partners.

While your journey is ultimately guided by the soul, you have free will and the gift of choice within your human experience, and there are many twists and turns to keep you surrendered to its ever-unfolding path.

THE TIME WOUND

How many of us, at some point along our journey, wish we could have a second chance to meet our counterparts without the triggering and challenges we face during our ascension? I know I do! It's what I call the Time Wound—a common fear of not having enough time or that we've lost time.

I'll never forget being at my counterpart's house one evening and picking up a picture of him from high school. I felt like I was looking at a stranger and the beloved all at once because I recognized him, having known him since elementary school, but I also didn't. Aside from my vivid dreams of us crossing paths in the hallways or locking eyes over the crowded cafeteria at lunch, I don't remember seeing him at all. It was like a veil had fallen over my vision, similar to my experience in New York when my best friend began talking about Twin Flames. I was blocked from any encounter with him once we parted ways in the fourth grade. He was there—of course, he was, and I was holding a picture to prove it. But it would be another fifteen years until we would become anything more than classmates drifting past each other in the halls.

I asked him once if he remembered seeing me in school because I couldn't understand how our paths never seemed to cross again from the time we were ten years old. I was admittedly in my own world back then—struggling with my health, participating in clubs and school events, and falling in (what I thought was) love for the first time. He told me, quite specifically, that he would notice me standing in the back of the auditorium where I was stationed as part of the tech crew for our musical productions. I burst into tears when he said this, my heart reeling in the devastation of so much lost time together. I couldn't wrap my head around the fact that *I never saw him*—at least, not consciously so—and while I thought I understood it from the energetic perspective that we still had soul contracts to fulfill and lessons to learn on our individual paths, I've recently unveiled another layer that's changed everything.

Writing this book has been a healing journey in and of itself, as reflecting on my experiences and putting our channelings into this organizational framework has allowed me to explore pieces of a puzzle I've held in my hand but never could quite place. Throughout my ascension with my counterpart, I've reflected on the interwoven threads of our lives and how this invisible string always seemed to connect us, drawing us close no matter where we were. I was reminded of our meeting as children—when he tried to show me the thread that tied our hearts together, when he seemed to love me first. He once admitted he'd always been in the background of my life, and he knew we would one day mean more to each other. I was dumbfounded, wondering if he wasn't always waiting for me as I'd been unconsciously waiting for him.

Why couldn't I see it? Why wasn't I ready for it? How could I let so much time pass between us?

I carried this Time Wound with me as layers wrapped around my heart that, over the years, I would return to, unraveling bit by bit with each revelation and subsequent healing. Just a few days ago, I was once again brought to that fourth-grade classroom—ready to dive deeper into this internal excavation than I've ever gone, ready to admit what I couldn't before.

I was the initial runner.

I was running away when he bravely shared his heart in elementary school. I was running away when I blocked myself from seeing him in the remaining school years together. I was running away when, after our first coffee date, I told him I needed to pull back from our frequent conversations because I was afraid of getting too attached.

It wasn't until that night at the diner—when our eyes locked and lit up and I intuitively knew I would keep my heart open wherever it led—that I finally stopped running away from him and from myself.

It felt like we'd found each other again. It was a chance to get it right. In hindsight, this is likely what activated my chaser energy and unlocked the runner-chaser dynamic wherein the roles reversed as we began our ascension. The sudden depth of feeling and intuitive heart pull opened stale wounds as I initially tried to box the connection into the old relationship paradigm. This only seemed to perpetuate the runner-chaser template within the Time Wound.

I always have compassion for those on this journey—you don't know what you don't know, and we have to forgive ourselves for those past states of unconsciousness as we learn, heal, and grow. Not until our ascension do we realize Time, naturally fluid and non-linear, is a human construct built into our everyday lives, and through our healing, we're constantly reshaping and rewriting old timelines until the present moment is our point of creative power. Still, it doesn't negate the lived, human experience, and boy, was I feeling the shame and regret of those years when we were so close yet seemingly so far apart!

Time, itself, is its own separation wound.

It's in your union that the runner-chaser template gets rewritten and the Time Wound heals and comes to a close. It's here you have a "second chance" to return to the beginning, only this time with a higher-level of consciousness and understanding, co-creating with your partner and navigating your ascension journey together.

THE SOULMATE PATH

Some of you will experience an unfolding of your higher-heart journey while already in partnership, such as marriages or other committed relationships, or with new connections in the form of platonic or romantic soulmate energy resonating as karmic soulmates or high-vibrational soulmate/counterpart connections, depending on your specific scenario. Remember, these are all labels. What's important is how the connections energetically feel.

These connections help you heal from previous experiences as you continue your soul growth, particularly through learning to embody conscious relationships. You also might experience a renewal of trust and forgiveness surrounding the external masculine or feminine. If you're in a marriage or committed relationship, for example, you might continue learning how to have healthier communication, deeper emotional intimacy, and more conscious interactions with your significant other. Similarly, if you're experiencing new connections, you'll meet people mirroring back the higher frequency of your personal transformation.

The inner work from your ascension journey has brought you to such a point that you're ready to experience the reflection of who you've become through your personal evolution. You'll know this not by the ego's assertion, "I'm ready! Bring on the relationship!" but by the divine surrender to the present moment and the peace and joy you feel from all you are and everything you have, not anything you want. This is your inner union.

Particularly for the Divine Feminine, as you heal your relationship with your inner masculine, you'll no longer attract or be attracted to distorted or wounded masculine connections. Instead, you'll attract and be attracted to conscious masculine archetypes that value and cherish the Divine Feminine energy. This soulmate path within your sacred union journey is part of your ascension, helping you remember and experience love in a way that honors you.

This path isn't for all, and everyone's journey will unfold in ways that are divinely designed and orchestrated for them. If you find yourself getting triggered at the thought of a new connection despite a lack of physical interaction or commitment with your counterpart, go within to see where threads of attachment, co-dependency, and expectation might still be active. Where are you still focused on your counterpart versus yourself? Where are you still attached to a particular blueprint for your union? The soulmate path isn't meant to replace your connection or detract from your inner knowing; however, this is where acceptance and surrender are necessary for your journey.

You're never meant to place yourself in a holding pattern, particularly where there's no mutual understanding or expression of commitment, as your human experience matters, too. I'll put it bluntly: if there's no communication, there's no relationship. That's not to say there isn't an *energetic connection*. Particularly for Twin Flames, this is, above all, a spiritual partnership. However, a relationship is one in which two people develop intimacy, communicate intentions, and grow together in some kind of established commitment based in reciprocated love. This is where your acceptance and surrender come in. As you reach a certain stage of your journey, you find you can hold within your heart unconditional love for your counterpart, but loving yourself in that same energy—and just *a little bit* more—allows for your human journey to continue instead of waiting for someone to communicate or offer commitment to you. In this respect, you're committing to and honoring yourself.

This is precisely what the sacred union path of ascension is all about, and your counterpart is your ultimate catalyst and boldest reflection. Your Twin Flame, at the highest energetic level and being one soul with you, *wants* you to grow and expand in your love for yourself, and part of your expansion might mean experiencing other connections.

There's a stark difference between seeking out new connections because of resentment towards your counterpart and being open to where your journey is guiding you, even if the journey looks a little different than you thought it would. The first is a distorted energy where you're acting out of your wounded nature. The second is a state of surrender where you're anchored into faith and self-love. With the latter, you intuitively know this is still your journey to union, even if that journey unexpectedly takes you along the soulmate path.

The soulmate path doesn't have to include romantic relationships, and it doesn't mean your counterpart isn't your counterpart. By opening your heart to every possibility, you're releasing your attachment to the human expectation and allowing yourself to surrender more to the soul's guidance. Many truths can co-exist at once, and there's often more happening energetically than our human experience shows us. You can know someone's your Twin Flame and hold the space for your connection while pursuing your life in the way your heart guides you.

You and your counterpart have a mission here on Earth, and no matter how your physical reality looks, you're always supporting each other in that mission. Imagine creating a beautiful garden where you're busy planting seeds in one corner while your partner works in the other. If you're constantly focused on their corner—what flowers are they planting, are the seeds growing, do they need better soil or more sunshine or water—you're only neglecting yourself by pulling energy away from the flowers you're trying to grow. But here's the thing—it's always the same, one garden! As your journey evolves, you learn that by focusing on your corner and trusting your counterpart to be focused on theirs, a beautiful, blossoming garden is created. In union, you can step back and admire what you've grown individually so you can continue to cultivate together.

You and your counterpart, as one soul, are always guided in your sacred union, and everyone and everything plays a part along its path. Soulmates and karmic connections come into our lives temporarily or with longevity to reflect our growth and help us further expand. They might also join our journey as we heal any karma within the Twin Flame connection itself from when you were both in your unconscious states. For example, if unconscious patterns continue to play out between you and your counterpart, the soul might orchestrate a separation for the energy to be cleared and the pattern to be shifted, especially if you only seem to perpetuate the cycles together. This is where soulmates or karmic-soulmate connections step forward to help with the healing and reflect further soul growth.

As I began to embody my Higher-Heart Ascension, I experienced surprising new soul connections stepping forth to reflect my inner transformation—all by divine orchestration, I might add! Some were kindred friendships that participated in my life briefly, and some are long-lasting soulmates who have helped me evolve to a higher level of my journey. Many of these connections were men mirroring my healing within my inner masculine energy, and while purely platonic, they've reflected my values of conscious effort, clear and direct communication, and honesty and transparency. Through our interactions, they've also shown me how I was trusting my own energy and intuition, what my boundaries were and how to comfortably affirm them, and where I was still attracting old patterns in connections. In each instance, their masculine presence facilitated a further shift from repeating cycles.

It's not just the masculine energy that's reflected in our transformation. In November 2022, I was introduced to my personal trainer—who I call my physical therapist (or just plain therapist for how I feel after leaving one of our sessions!). I'd spent so much of my journey working on my emotional healing that now I wanted to focus on my physical health, particularly as I was in the middle of another relapse with Lyme disease. My trainer and I instantly clicked, as she's incredibly intuitive and energetically inclined, and over the years of working with her, she's become part of my soul family. Through movement therapy and conscious activity, I've sifted through deep and heavy emotions while learning how to express myself in the flow of my Divine Feminine energy.

Each connection I've encountered along my journey has reflected back to me my personal evolution in encouraging and supportive ways. This is what the soulmate path is all about. New connections don't have to be life partners or romantic relationships—although that's certainly a choice. The soulmate path is one of healing and persistent expansion, and while you'll continue to grow energetically with your Twin Flame, you're meant to experience *life*, too.

Don't keep yourself stuck in the pain and suffering of a journey that's meant to guide you home to peace and joy. Open your heart to love in all its many forms. Be the love for your beloved.

RECOGNIZING REUNION

When you come into physical reunion or reconciliation with your sacred partner—whether this is your catalyst counterpart or a new ascension partner—it will feel like you're starting your journey all over again. In many ways, you are—as new versions of yourselves in a higher frequency, a more conscious state of awareness, and with so many more spiritual tools and resources at your disposal. You won't experience the same tension and friction as in the past because you'll no longer be acting out of your unconscious patterns. Reunion becomes a process of communicating or spending time with each other as your energies realign.

Reunion doesn't mean there won't be conflict or challenges, especially as you anchor your union into a physical relationship. As much as I want to say otherwise, being the romantic that I am, it's just not realistic. However, because you've both done the inner work and are acting in conscious embodiment, you'll now be able to sustain your physical union. Rather than working against each other in the resistance of your triggers, you'll be working with each other for greater healing, harmony, and growth in the reflection of your unconditional love.

You and your counterpart will continue to evolve, individually and together, from a new recognition of conscious connection versus repeating pain patterns. You might even find yourself detaching from the journey as you knew it—no longer needing to analyze your experiences or actively seek support as often. Fueled by your innate connection to GodSource, your continued ascension transforms into an organic process as you become the bridge and ground your spiritual essence into your human being.

CREATING SPACE FOR PHYSICAL UNION

Your partner is constantly catalyzing you towards more soul growth and expansion, even in union. This is the role you play for each other within the soul's expression of unconditional love. Throughout your journey, you're coming home to yourself (as one soul) and each other (in human form) in that love, but it's important to stay focused on what you, individually, are creating. Your passions, your purpose, and how you express these in your physical world with your career, friendships, family, hobbies, and more is what makes space for your partner's gifts and everything they bring to the connection so you can then decide what you wish to create together from this new starting point.

Trying to control or manage your physical union pulls you back into old, unconscious patterns and pushes the connection away. You're forgetting you already are in union! You always have been and always will be. Controlling, forcing, manipulating, or managing any aspect of your sacred relationship creates a separation, as you're looking outside of yourself for what you already have. As Rumi famously says, "What you seek is seeking you," or, as we recently channeled, "What you're seeking you already are." Anything less than divine surrender only creates resistance.

This doesn't mean you're a passive participant in your life. You're not waiting for the phone to ring or praying to the Universe that you'll bump into each other. Come on, of course not! You're an empowered being now who has better things to do with their time—a whole life to live, a world to explore, and a hell of a lot of energetic ass to kick.

(Are we feeling feisty yet?)

What surrender does mean is you're letting it be. *Letting it be.* It has a certain sigh of relief about it, doesn't it? Take a couple of deep breaths and relax your body, repeating that phrase… *Let it be, let it be, let it be.* See how your body surrenders? This is your Divine Feminine energy sinking into the secure container of the Divine Masculine—we'll talk more about him in the next section.

Maintain your independence and stay focused on your journey as you transmute any old energies that pop up, especially as they relate to the past. Utilize the tools and resources from your journey, going back to the basics if necessary, to remember how you've grown and how far you've come in your embodiment of the sacred.

We've said it a hundred times, and we'll say it once more: this journey is a process, so allow the process to unfold even as the physical manifests in unexpected ways. What's happening on the physical plane isn't all there is—so much more is aligning energetically in this spiritual connection. Trust in your heart and intuition while holding space for and accepting what's presenting in the physical. What might look like small steps—and even regressions in some cases—are actually energetic leaps forward.

Tips For Reunion & Reconciliation

As I'm writing this book, I've been in touch with several clients who have unexpectedly reunited or had significant communication with their Twin Flame or sacred partner. While this journey continues to evolve, we've channeled some additional support for those experiencing this initial stage of physical union.

∞ Don't rush the process. The Divine Feminine holds the vision and can see the broader perspective, or "blueprint," of this journey, which might lead to some impatience and frustration. This is where your practice of divine surrender is so important and where your faith in the masculine energy is anchored. Remember, the Divine Masculine is conscious in their own right. The Divine Feminine leads energetically through her inner work, but the Divine Masculine intuitively knows when it's time to put that into action in the physical based on your growth and his. Focus on your inner feminine and masculine energies to anchor in more of this trust and continue to affirm healthy boundaries and self-love.

∞ Don't compare your journey. Your sacred union is just that—*sacred* to you and your counterpart, and while you may be part of a collective having similar experiences, your journey is still yours and only yours. Union isn't a destination or goal to achieve. It's something you remember within you, as part of you. Don't look to anyone else's experience as a barometer for where you are on your journey. Instead, trust that your path is unfolding in the way that's perfect for you—because it's orchestrated by you! Everything is energy and alignment, and your inner work creates the shifts and leads the way.

∞ Keep trusting your intuition. Coming into physical reunion and establishing your sacred relationship might look a little chaotic on the surface. But not everything is as it seems along this journey, especially when it comes to our material world. Looking for "evidence" in your physical life will only distract you from your inner knowing and pull you out of alignment. Ground your inner masculine energy to create safety and security within and stay anchored into the present moment—this will help you refrain from falling into fears, which are only reflections of your own uncertainty.

∞ Don't be afraid of separation. This is the key to anchoring in and sustaining your union. It might seem a little counter-intuitive, but remember this is a journey full of paradoxes. The fear of separation creates separation because you're feeding into an illusion that's the opposite of what you desire. As you begin your physical relationship, you're forming a more stable foundation than you had in the past—one that's built on authenticity, honoring of each other, and conscious connection. You're both different versions than you used to be, and you might want to get to know each other again in this new energy. There might also be some periods of "separation" as you energetically recalibrate and reestablish your connection, but this is part of the process. Continue to do the inner work for any fears, beliefs, or patterns that crop up.

Your sacred union is the story of your evolution. It's the home-coming to love within the soul that ripples outwards in reflections of the world around you. It's the recognition of oneness of which our existence was born. Nothing is ever separate. Your sacred union is, and always has been, an intrinsic part of you.

You've always been in union.

CHAPTER EIGHT
SATISFYING THE SOUL

"We are all different expressions of one reality, different songs of
one singer, different dances of one dancer, different paintings—
but the painter is one."
– Osho

THE PROCESS GOES LIKE THIS: the more you heal and transform
within yourself and anchor in your inner union—the harmonization of the masculine and feminine polarities within you—the
more you see that reflected in the healing and transformation
with your embodied counterpart in outer physical union. But, as
we've learned, there's so much more to this journey than a physical
relationship. Your connection activates your spiritual ascension—a
deepening of your connection to yourself and God—while leading
you to your spiritual mission in service to humanity.

Humanity itself is complex, and through our ascension, we
learn that life is a paradox. We might feel conflicted as we transition between realms of consciousness, having trouble reconciling
instances of harm and injustice and moments of kindness and beauty,
but this is where your journey matters. You're opening to a greater
love for humanity with the ability to channel that love into positive
change, healing and evolving the planet in even the subtlest ways.

I'm of the belief that part of our soul mission is simply embodying more love in our everyday lives. In my book *Daybreak: Daily*

Messages to Illuminate Your Spiritual Life, one of our channeled messages reads: "Your mission is first and foremost to be the truest and most authentic version of yourself you can be. Through exuding the love that is the core essence of all you are, you then embody that within your physical, human experience as part of your double mission…"

In short, you make a difference in the world just by being in it.

The way you express yourself as love can play itself out in a thousand different ways. Perhaps you're guided to activism and being a voice for the voiceless, or you're inventing something that will benefit future generations, or you're bringing more intuition to rigid systems, much like Laura and her corporate career in our example in Chapter Two. You might change career tracks entirely to something more aligned with your values, or explore a hobby that lights you up and brings joy to others, or transfer locations to an environment more soothing to your soul. You might raise a family or expand your friend group or welcome an animal into its forever home.

Personally, I never expected to be doing the spiritual work that's been central to my life for the better part of a decade now, though I can see how every step of my life has, in some way, played a role in building towards this greater mission of service to others. My novels are stories of humanity, and my greatest joy when writing is sharing universal experiences so readers connect to parts of themselves they may have forgotten. My non-profit was created with this same purpose in mind: to advocate for the emotional well-being of patients and their caregivers, ensuring they know their voices are heard and their lives matter. This continues as part of my mission for *Susan Dawn Spiritual Connections* and is why I share certain aspects of my personal story so openly—in a time of massive confusion and emotional isolation, it's helpful to know we're not alone in our experiences, particularly when those experiences are so dang phenomenal.

When I was debating traditional publishing for my first full-length novel, *The Last Letter*, I reached out to a literary agent who had become a friend and mentor over the years, explaining that I felt a little lost on the publishing path. I didn't want to wait the many years publishing can take, and I didn't want to reimagine the story for an ever-changing market as I knew editors would suggest. I wanted to tell a story—my story—in such a way that it would create awareness for chronic illness and reassure patients they weren't alone in their experiences. She responded with something I'll never forget:

"There are people out there who will need this," she wrote, encouraging my decision to publish through my independent imprint. "They'll find you in the middle of the night, and you'll be lighting candles in a dark world."

I believe we're all lighting candles in the dark in our own way.

Much like your connection to God, your purpose is personal to you as an expression of your unique soul, and your sacred relationship will support and complement that purpose. Ultimately, it doesn't matter what you choose for your job or external mission. As long as you're aligned with your passion, which is an extension of your heart, your mission goes beyond the physicality of a career. The real question is, how are you embodying your truth? How are you exuding love? How are you expressing your authentic self? Whatever you choose from the human perspective, do it because you love it, because your heart calls you to it, and allow yourself to keep evolving with it.

You and your counterpart have a mission together, and that mission is pure love. You might express that mission in the form of a relationship, having a family together, traveling together, or starting a business together—or all of it!—or you might have your individual experiences but be in conscious support of one another. Each couple's path will look different, but the most important aspect is that you're reflecting love to yourself, to each other, and to the world. This is how we change the world.

Don't force your mission or seek out your purpose if you're unaware of it yet. It will find you as you continue on your path, as it will naturally coincide with your personal journey and converge with your counterpart's. Keep exploring what lights you up, what brings you joy, and what ignites a passion within you. These are the very foundations of your soul's mission.

HUMANITY'S BRIDGE

Your ascension journey will likely be the hardest experience you'll ever encounter, which is why I always emphasize kindness, compassion, and patience for yourself and others. You don't know what you don't know when you didn't know it, and it's useless to be hard on yourself for the previous levels of consciousness in which you were operating or the actions or beliefs you held then. Again, that version of you served a purpose, so love and embrace that version of yourself as once being part of yourself! Everything in the Universe is a building block, and all is interconnected, including your soul's journey.

This is, after all, evolution.

While the planet is collectively ascending, not everyone will be consciously aware of these timeline shifts and energetic transformations. Still, everyone has their part as they journey on their individual paths. Even those playing the role of opposition are catalysts for ascension from the soul's perspective—though, it doesn't mean we have to like it from the human point of view! Looking at this from the wider lens of the soul's journey, however, we can see how certain individuals or groups of people become catalysts for change. From chaos comes order, and from destruction comes creation. Everything is cyclical, and everything serves its purpose.

Conscious awareness begets a certain responsibility. It can be challenging, even frustrating, to reach new levels of consciousness through your inner work and wish for others to share the same experience. But you're not responsible for others' journeys. You are, however, responsible for your own as you lead by example while continuing to learn and grow. This is where you surrender control and focus on the path you're co-creating with the world around you. This is where you hold space for loved ones and the greater collective. This is where you compassionately meet others where they are by seeing beyond the human ego to the soul within.

This is the embodiment of the Christ-Sophia consciousness.

The Christ-Sophia consciousness is a holy template of unconditional love in the union of the masculine and feminine principles. The more each of us embodies this template through our individual ascension, the more we anchor new energetic codes within the collective consciousness here on Earth.

Inscribed in stone above the entrance to the Temple of Apollo at Delphi, known in part for the Oracle of Delphi, is the phrase, *know thyself.* To know yourself is to connect to the soul essence—the Divine core—of all you are. It's here we return to wholeness, calling back any fragmented aspects across lifetimes, and it's here, anchoring into the present time and space, that the collective energy shifts. This embodiment recognizes the seed of life—the eternal interconnectedness of all things. Unity consciousness isn't just a fantasy or concept but a living, breathing way of being.

Think back to who you thought you were before your ascension journey began. Consider your heart, your mind, your very life. How much has changed? Who have you become? How do you view life or the Universe now, and how different is it from what it was before?

Last year, I experienced a mild Lyme disease relapse. I stared at the results of my blood test and began to cry in my doctor's office, unable to keep the tears at bay—a trauma response of having experienced the same scenario twice before. Within minutes, I felt my breath calm and peace enter my heart. This was simply the residue of old trauma coming to the surface, I realized. I'd been here before, and even though I'd experienced so much pain and suffering from that very first Lyme diagnosis, this wasn't then, and I wasn't the same person now. Even my physical life looked starkly different—I had a new naturopath, a personal trainer, and a nutritionist, and I was less stressed as I was able to set my own hours through my business to better care for my body and what it needed. More than that, my health itself wasn't where it was over a decade ago, nor was my emotional capacity or mental state. Even though a similar experience was presenting itself, it wasn't the same because I was different.

Such is your ascension journey. As you rise in consciousness, you reach a new level of yourself, which reflects in your life. Where you might have spiraled for days, weeks, months due to comparable situations or challenges from your past, now you're embodying a new version of yourself so that all those old coping mechanisms simply don't work anymore. The old you is still there—the memory of who you used to be and all the wisdom you've learned (and earned) carried with you—but you're no longer attached to the story or emotions. Again, it's like a video game—with each save, there's always a new starting point, and you never fully return to the level before it.

We're collectively ascending into a new way of being within this human being. Out of the division and into more harmony, out of the fear and into more love, out of the lack and into more abundance as we recognize everything is one with the Universe, and we're one with everything around us.

This is part of the soul's mission and why you're united with your Twin Flame or sacred partner in this present time—to assist in the planet's ascension. It's why the old forms of relationship, particularly karmic connections, are giving way to sacred unions. The more we embody our higher-selves, the more we embrace the new template of unconditional love.

RECALLING THE GODSPARK

What you experience on your individual ascension journey or in your counterpart connection is also seen on a greater, collective scale within the polarities as a whole. Energy is becoming balanced, harmony is being restored, and the masculine and feminine principles are reaching a tipping point wherein mutual honor and respect must be recognized.

Through your divine partnership, you're helping to birth a new collective consciousness—the Christ-Sophia consciousness. It's a return to the garden, a resurrection of the sacred, and a remembrance of our oneness with God and all as part of God. GodSource isn't just the masculine principle—a notion that's been accepted for centuries, particularly in secular religion, in order to manipulate and control through feminine suppression. Rather, it's the eternal union of the masculine and feminine that has never been and never will be separate.

You and your counterpart are infinite in your connection to the Universe as love itself. When you remember your union, a trinity with God is formed. In the early years of my channeling, I was shown this through the symbol of a triangle with GodSource at the apex and the Divine Masculine and Divine Feminine at each connecting point. However, the more I continued on my journey, the more I understood that while the triangle was a perfectly fine foundation for understanding the trinity energy, there were still elements of separation.

I was then shown the Three of Cups in a non-traditional tarot deck where two cups, both containing the same substance, pour into a third, similar to what's replicated here:

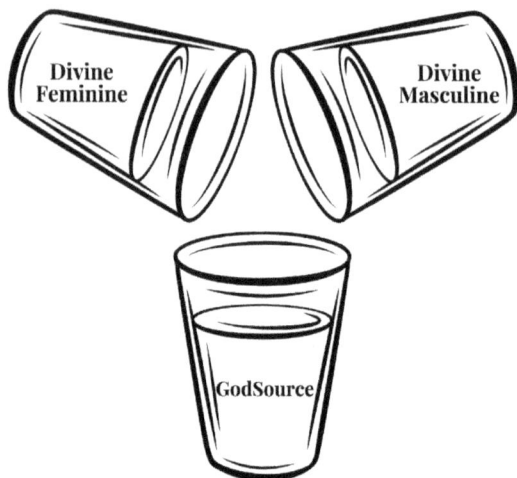

The two cups, as the Divine Masculine and Divine Feminine polarities, merge with the third such that there is no separation—not even the illusion of it. This is the essence of your inner union. You're one with GodSource, one with your counterpart, and one with yourself. You've anchored within you this understanding as a perfect, unshakable truth that the union reflected within you reflects in oneness with all.

You've experienced duality throughout many lifetimes so that you might know oneness with all living consciousness. The dualistic viewpoint of your past experiences was one of separation. Now, you're remembering union as a new gateway for creation.

It's here you recall the Godspark within you.

THE TWIN FLAME
COSMIC EFFECT

Stepping into your highest embodiment and personal empowerment shifts the collective consciousness. That embodiment
then expresses itself in your physical world through your human
mission; however, there's a greater energetic purpose for you and
your sacred relationship that has an unimaginable cosmic effect.

Many years ago, during one of my earliest channelings, I was
shown a vision of a shadow covering the Earth. I was told it had
been this way for millennia as an ongoing war between the light
and dark and that there was rarely a time when we knew pure,
unconditional love. This resulted from the fall in consciousness,
or stepping out of the garden.

Through your inner shift into higher consciousness, you
become an open vessel for more light. This is, in part and on the
highest level, why you're clearing out all of those heavy, dense
energies that I like to call soul sludge—so that more light can
be experienced. As part of your sacred union path of ascension,
you're catalyzed to this inner transformation through your physical
counterpart, whom you recognize as the beloved and who shows
you that you, yourself, are beloved.

Can we take a moment to acknowledge how profound this is?
For centuries, we've been conditioned to seek outside of ourselves
for our value and taught that loving ourselves is selfish. How radical
it is to then recognize yourself as the beloved! Loving yourself
changes the whole game. It's what lifts the shadow. It's what creates
a revolution.

Your journey is part of an internal revolution with energetic
ripple effects far beyond your human experience. In your inner
union, you recognize yourself in the beloved and the beloved within
you. You remember there is and never has been separation and
that you're one with all. You become the divine template of the

healer-warrior, standing in your soul's truth and embodying inner peace and unconditional love.

When Twin Flames join together in this sacred honoring of each other through the powerful symbol of love that is your union, there's a burst of pure cosmic energy—an indescribable force of light that ricochets across the Universe.

Can you feel it now stirring within your heartspace, in the very seat of your soul? You've experienced the whispers of it throughout your life. You felt the spark of it when you met your Twin Flame, when you were activated to your ascension journey. You've begun to embody this in your everyday experience. It's your divine remembrance in the power of God's love—a love that exists within you, as you.

This cosmic effect was shown to me as a supernova—a Big Bang energy with such magnitude that it births new worlds. Similar to when two bodies merge in the sacred intimacy of physical union, so, too, does energetic union lead to an explosion of cosmic creation. Darkness, having nowhere to hide, surrenders to light, and that light collapses timelines and dimensions to return us to the garden from which we never truly left.

THE UNITY CODE

Union upholds the balance of the Universe as the intersection of matter and energy, masculine and feminine. As these unions collectively take place, you lead the way in birthing a new template of love in sacred relationships and a new world of oneness in conscious creation. No longer are you fragmented, split from the wholeness of yourself and GodSource. Shifting into higher consciousness, you access the infinite nature of your divine blueprint and recognize the truth of this oneness, lifting the veil to see beyond the limited perceptions of all you think you know.

The modern world is in a feverish state of disorder, with a dismantling of old structures and an examination of previously-held systemic beliefs. However, it's the cycle of life and the inherent nature of our ascension that from destruction comes creation, from endings come new beginnings. This chaos is the tipping point for change.

Joining together with your Twin Flame or sacred partner, or even simply experiencing this union within yourself, sets the foundation for a collective rebirth and plants the seeds for generations to come. Everything is interconnected in this way. There's not one thing in this world that isn't part of the whole, that doesn't serve a purpose, and your path unfolds in divine accordance.

You are the embodiment of higher consciousness, becoming the living bridge of spiritual essence and human being.

You are the template of unconditional love, carrying the imprint of your sacred union ascension journey with you.

You are The Unity Code.

CHAPTER NINE
THE CONSCIOUS CONNECTION

"He who experiences the unity of life sees his own self in all
beings, and all beings in his own self..."
– *The Bhagavad Gita*

IT'S MY HOPE THAT YOU'VE been considering the teachings in this
book for yourself and your inner Divine Masculine and Divine
Feminine energies as much as for your sacred relationship. If not,
give it another read and see if anything shifts for you! Inner union
is a key component of any conscious connection. Claim that energy
back and empower yourself by seeing what it unlocks for you.

The inner work on this journey hasn't been easy. You've
screamed. You've cried. You've raged. The world is screaming
and raging now as it undergoes its own collective process. But
revolution is transformation, and transformation is a revolution.
Everyone—every single soul incarnated on this planet at this
pivotal moment—plays a role in the process.

Want to know a secret?

No one ever really knows what they're doing, especially when
starting out on a journey as crazy and wild as spiritual ascension!
But you learn. You forgive yourself for what you didn't know, and
you try to do better. You fall and break down, and you get back
up. You find the courage to continue or the strength to start over.

You trust.

You listen and pay attention. You tune into your inner knowing and higher guidance. You stay true to who you are. You embody your spiritual center but don't forget your human heart.

And you grow, you grow, you grow.

Every moment of your ascension journey will teach you, but the lessons aren't only applied to your relationship with your counterpart. They contain valuable wisdom for the whole of your life. Your sacred union is a byproduct of establishing a sacred relationship with yourself.

As you bear witness to your emotions without crafting a story, you create space in your heart to hold others' experiences without judgment or prejudice. As you access the shadow parts of yourself, you embrace more compassion for those around you. As you show yourself more grace and love, you set a new standard for grace and love in the world.

NURTURING THE ROOTS

Conscious connection isn't just about our relationships with other people. It's our relationship with ourselves, with our material world, and with the Universe itself. Connection permeates everything, and the more we allow ourselves to grow into the best version of who we are now from who we used to be, the more we see this reflected as a powerful ripple effect in our lives. But change isn't easy, and we're perfectly imperfect. We need to grant ourselves this grace as we continue to evolve.

When I was younger, I viewed relationships through a pretty naïve lens. I used to believe love was all that mattered—as long as you have love, you can get through anything. I still believe this to a degree, but I've since realized there's more to healthy relationships. Yes, love is all you need because, beneath it all, love is all there is. But love is also the foundation—the roots of a tree from which branches of trust, integrity, communication, and emotional intimacy are formed. Infected branches can be mended, but if the roots are decayed, the whole tree suffers.

In a relationship, the seed is planted by two people, with each individual contributing to its growth. If we water the seed with our old templates of co-dependency, insecurity, mistrust, and apathy, the tree won't mature. But if we're mindful of our efforts by recognizing how we tend to ourselves and each other, the roots spread—deep and lasting—and the branches become strong and supportive.

The seeds of our connections can only thrive when all aspects are consciously nourished. As we evolve, we're called to plant healthier gardens.

Starting with ourselves.

CREATING THE TRINITY

Your sacred relationship with your counterpart provides an example of healthy connection without the toxic templates of co-dependency, self-abandonment, and conditional love—among all the other patterns and beliefs we heal and clear along our journey. A secure container is created for the connection itself in which you both can embody your full self-expression, encouraging each other in your soul growth and in your humanness. In times of conflict, you learn to self-soothe and regulate your individual nervous systems while working together to find solutions for mutual repair and reconnection. Communication centers around bids for emotional intimacy and allows for sharing emotions and experiences without defensiveness or blame. With these tenets, in the continued freedom of your individuality, your relationship develops into the unifying "we."

This third energy, your sacred relationship, becomes a place for you and your counterpart to co-create your dreams in the way that best suits your partnership. Maybe you desire marriage in a traditional family structure, or maybe you're co-parenting as part of a blended family. Perhaps you want to travel with your children and show them the world, or you and your partner want to raise your kids within a supportive community. Maybe you don't want children at all but aspire to build a business or work together in some established way.

Whatever your dreams with your counterpart, they serve a purpose. The more you put into practice and apply everything you've learned throughout your journey to your sacred relationship, the more those dreams are created within the new template of higher consciousness.

PUTTING IT INTO PRACTICE

Remember these four core tenets for conscious connecting:

∞ Personal responsibility. Taking accountability for your emotions, reactions, and behaviors helps you step into your personal autonomy as you remember you're in charge of your life and only your life. Through individual responsibility, you empower yourself to make choices that are self-honoring while also honoring another, which supports healthier decisions and helps you connect more mindfully to your partner and the world around you—a world that you, yourself, are co-creating.

∞ Forgiveness. Forgiveness is a healing energy that has the capacity to change not only your life, but the lives of those around you as an act of love that allows for transformation. When you invite forgiveness into your relationship, you begin a cycle of repair, renewal, and reconnection. Forgiveness requires letting go of shame and blame, including self-blame, while taking personal responsibility. Use the Ho'oponopono prayer in Chapter Five to begin practicing forgiveness for yourself and others.

∞ Authenticity. You can't consciously connect with another unless you're consciously connected to yourself. This means becoming intimately aware of your emotions, staying grounded in your physical body, and being in tune with your soul. In this space of knowing yourself, you embrace the full, embodied expression of who you are without reservation, shame, guilt, or fear. You're a beautiful, unique aspect of GodSource energy, and your authentic expression of that energy is a beacon of light in this world. Remembering this and remaining connected to your authentic self reflects genuine connections and experiences in your life.

∞ Communication. Conscious communication builds trust, nurtures intimacy, and repairs and restores moments of disconnection within a relationship. By fostering an environment where you and your partner can freely express yourselves and share your experiences without blame or judgment, you're creating a safe space for your relationship to grow. Conscious communication is the bridge that deepens the bonds we share.

It's easy, especially within the spiritual community, to put divine partnerships on a pedestal and idealize the relationship.

Spiritual relationships are sacred, but sacredness doesn't mean perfection—we're still human, and being human means allowing for a wide range of emotions and experiences. Relationships then become a conscious container of intimacy and security for both our human expression and spiritual growth.

CHAPTER TEN
NAVIGATING ASCENSION

"Why struggle to open a door between us when the whole
world is an illusion?"
– Rumi

"WHY DO YOU THINK PEOPLE *give up,*" *he asks me.*

*I don't want to have this conversation. I want to shut down—to just
listen to music and read my book and forget this whole journey. But I can
feel his smile more than I can see it in my mind. It's gentle. Patient. Kind.*

"You know that's not possible, dear one."

*"It's because they're tired," I answer, a little bitterly. "It's because
they don't want to be in pain anymore."*

*I don't say what I really want to say: it's because they've been tested
and broken down, and how many times are we meant to rise? How
many times are we meant to build ourselves back up? How many times
are we meant to hear about the blessings when the heart is hurting in
this moment, now?*

I don't say this, but he knows. Of course, he does.

*He waits for my surrender. I sigh. I feel defeated today, but I know
what he's going to say—that it's just a moment. That I'm transforming,
healing, ascending. That he's so proud of me. That tomorrow will be
better. But I don't need tomorrow. I need now.*

*"It's because they don't turn to me," he says finally. His words
surprise me. They shouldn't, but they do. "You think you have to carry*

it all on your own, but that's not why you were created. That's not what you're here to experience. That was my job. Put down the weight of all you've been carrying; the time of self-punishment is over. I am as I always have been, here to lift you from your burdens.

"People give up," he continues, "because they think they're alone. *They forget to reach out—to others, to me. And in their solitude, they forget the strength of their own heart, the power of their spirit that they themselves yield. They forget, so lost in their humanness, how connected they are to everything around them, most of all to each other. Most of all to me."*

I don't know what to say, but I know I don't have to say anything. He smiles gently and brushes a kiss against my forehead.

"Tomorrow will be better, dear one," he says. "Don't give up on *this moment now. This is where you are. This is where I am. This is where you'll begin to rise again."*

I wrote the above passage in 2019 at the height of my ascension journey, healing trauma and deconstructing beliefs during a near-constant cycle of soul growth that had become my life's focus for the greater part of two years. I was exhausted and jaded from everything I'd been through and yet motivated to keep going, spurred onwards by changes I could feel within myself that kept reflecting in my physical world. This cathartic conversation, channeled during a journaling session, served as a reminder of our indomitable spirit and infinite connection. Sharing it now, these many years later, I recognize it as a sacred promise for our ascension.

We never fully see ourselves when we're in the midst of radical transformation. How can we? We're in between versions of ourselves, letting go of who we used to be to become more of who we are. Maybe this is why we struggle, why we resist. Maybe this is why we're so often brought to our knees—because we find comfort in the familiar, but we're not meant to stay there. It's reminiscent of the story of the caterpillar turning into the butterfly, breaking down its DNA to develop into something altogether new. Does the caterpillar know she's transforming? Or does she allow herself the breakdown without knowing the butterfly she's becoming. Perhaps it's in her very surrender that she activates the divine codes of her metamorphosis, liberating herself from what she was into the fully formed creation of what she was always designed to be.

The world is ascending through its own metamorphosis now, but just like we forget about the caterpillar once it becomes the butterfly, the world won't know the story of our personal transformation and how we're clearing the past to create future timelines. It won't know the courage you claimed as you dove into the recesses of yourself, drowning in centuries-old programming in order to offer breath to new patterns and ways of being. It won't know the strength you needed as you faced yourself mirrored in another, burning away toxic templates to purify the heart back into unified love. It won't know the amount of trust you required to believe in the unseen or the force of love it entailed to keep your faith.

The world won't know. And that's OK.

You're changing the world right now with every habit you break, every pattern you shift, and every conscious choice that brings you closer to yourself and God. Of course, you feel a little jaded when you look at the state of the present world. Of course, you question if it matters. Of course, you wonder if you're even making a difference.

But consider the difference this journey has already made in you. You're not who used to be. You're growing, expanding, and the world grows and expands, too—even if we can't see the collective reflection just yet. Through your individual ascension, you're planting seeds for a garden that has no choice but to bloom.

Tomorrow is what we create today.

ASCENSION GUIDE

Energy Purges

With energetic purges come heightened emotions as we release past energies and clear outdated programs. This release can trigger a temporary emotional imbalance, which can lead to outbursts and upsurges in anger or grief (or varying degrees of each), depending on what's being released. Become an observer of the emotions you're feeling, and don't be afraid as you sit in the temporary discomfort of what you're feeling, knowing they won't last. These emotions are the release of stored energy that may have been suppressed for months or years, affecting your mental, spiritual, emotional, and physical life.

The more self-aware you are, the easier it is to navigate the ascension process in healthy and productive ways. Turn to a community, counselor, spiritual advisor, or trusted friend to help you hold space for this process. Use creative outlets such as writing or art to help you express your emotions. Practice stream-of-consciousness journaling to release the judgment and shame of the ego and let the energy flow. This is about the process, not perfection. Remember, you're not your thoughts or emotions.

You're safe. You're held. You're loved.

Dark Night Of The Soul

The Dark Night of the Soul is an illusion—or at least, the purging of illusion. It's a spiritual, sometimes existential crisis in which the internal world you knew becomes uprooted, and you're forced to face everything held within the subconscious as your egoic identity starts to break down. Dark Nights of the Soul are usually part of your awakening or ascension journey. This period of your life can feel like a void or disconnect from the reality you once knew, but it's meant to bring you deeper into the truth of yourself. It can be a paralyzing time of emotional upheaval and may impact your physical life. Bearing that all mental and physical health concerns are considered and alleviated, the Dark Night of the Soul is an initiation for inner transformation and spiritual growth.

As the saying goes, "Who you were before you went into the fire will not be who you are when you come out." The same goes for your Dark Night of the Soul. It's going through the proverbial fire to burn away the illusions of everything you believed you were and everything you thought the world was to return to your true nature of unconditional faith, love, and light. The Dark Night of the Soul is temporary and won't last forever. Turn to your spiritual guidance team and trusted friends, soul family, and community for support. Nurture yourself as best as possible, remembering that the sun always rises and so will you.

Learning Discernment

Your intuition is located in the seat of the soul. It's the voice of your higher consciousness that remains balanced, steadfast, and in an energy of love while providing support and direction. While the ego likes to shout and direct in fear as a method of self-preservation and centuries of serving as a survival mechanism ("Don't do that or this will happen!"), the soul is a whisper of love guiding you gently along your journey.

Discerning between the ego and the soul-self is a key part of trusting your intuition. This is why your connection to yourself is an integral aspect of your spiritual journey—the better you know yourself and the more aware you are, the better you can trust yourself over other influences.

When you live your life according to the actions of others versus your intuition ("He's doing that, so I should probably do this"), you're giving another power over yourself by not listening and trusting what is meant for *you*. This creates separation within yourself. While others can positively influence you through support, encouragement, and insight, trusting yourself and what resonates through following your intuition leads to your personal sovereignty and self-empowerment.

Learning to trust your intuition takes practice and patience, as it's a continuing process of self-discovery and personal connection. Using tools like oracle and tarot cards can help you hone these intuitive skills. To learn how to tune into your soul's truth using the art of intuitive tarot, check out my *Tarot in Translation* Online Course!

Energy Protection

We don't talk about this enough, but energy protection is one of the most crucial elements of your ascension journey. Your energy is your greatest commodity. In fact, you *are* energy, and in order to fully care for yourself, you have to prioritize your well-being, including invoking spiritual protection.

As we shift in frequency and embody higher consciousness, our light will shine on the shadows—even in our sacred relationships where we might feel our partner's energy, particularly as they navigate Dark Nights of the Soul and ego dissolutions. While we can have compassion for others and facilitate support where we can, we're not meant to take on the responsibility of another's journey or suffer with them. Our ascension teaches us how to heal through love, not through pain, and we can't hold space in that energy of love if we're engulfed in the same fear as the world around us.

Especially as you open up to your intuition and spiritual gifts, it becomes necessary to regularly clear, balance, and protect your energy in order to release any energy you might attach to unconsciously. Call upon your spirit team to protect your energy so you can continue your journey in peace and love, lighting the way for yourself and others.

Your spirit team consists of higher aspects of the one GodSource and is always with you. In fact, similar to your counterpart, your spirit team isn't separate from you or outside of yourself. When we mention listening to your intuition and trusting your inner guidance, know this includes your spirit team, which is always connected to God. While your spirit team might deliver some tough-love messages and guidance, they will never be fear-based, critical, or negative. God is your Source, and in communion with God, any energy brought forth from your spirit team will always be held in a container of love.

While tools such as sprays, candles, and herb bundles can be helpful, what's most important is your intention. There's power in your thoughts, and your intention is the key. Visualize surrounding yourself with pure golden or white light and use mantras and meditations to clear out any energetic debris. Reach out to trusted sources to help balance and clear negative energy if you're finding yourself in need of additional support.

The tenets of self-love in Chapter Six offer additional ways to honor your energy, including maintaining healthy boundaries and rest. Clearing your energy regularly can help you become more balanced and in tune with yourself and your environment. Explore our *Chakra Alignment Series* for powerful Light Language Transmissions to align you to your highest frequency as additional support.

Tips For Your Ascension Journey

+ Mindfulness Exercises: When the energy around you feels chaotic, practice being in a state of presence to find your balance.

- Breathwork: Your breath is your sacred connection to the Divine within you. Take deep, mindful breaths to connect to your higher heart.
- Rest: So much is experienced during ascension that the body, too, needs time to recharge and recalibrate along with the new energies. Allow yourself to rest or sleep as you need to.
- Grounding: Go for walks in nature, hug a tree or run your fingers through plant soil, take a shower or sea salt bath, or spend a few moments in direct sunlight.
- Move Your Body: Stagnant energy creates discord within the body. Dance, walk, exercise, stretch, and play to get the energy flowing again.
- Express Yourself: Emotions are energy. Express yourself and release your emotions in healthy, creative ways.

ANSWERING COMMON TWIN FLAME QUESTIONS

I'm feeling my partner's energy. What do I do?
You might, at times, feel a surge of energy as part of your partner's individual ascension journey. This is experienced as bursts of love and acceptance or an influx of anxiety, anger, or other similar emotion as they undergo Dark Nights of the Soul or ego dissolution. For some, you or your counterpart might be consciously aware of each other's energy while for others, you might feel their emotions as physical sensations or experience an activated dreamstate.

While we can hold space for our counterparts, we're not meant to assume their journey for them—can you imagine going through the experience of your ascension twice? In the conscious awareness of our Higher-Heart Ascension, we heal through love, not through pain, and we can't hold the light and be in an energy of love if we're in the same energy of illusion.

Tune into your own heartspace to discern whether the energy is yours. Clear and transmute what you can, and call upon your spirit team to protect your energy. This doesn't mean you're leaving your counterpart to fend for themselves—on the contrary, anchoring in your peace and love helps your counterpart heal, grow, and rise in their divine light. It's the love you have for each other that guides the way.

How do I know if they're really my Twin Flame?

Only you can tell, through your inner knowing, whether or not someone is your Twin Flame, and part of your ascension journey is learning discernment between your heart's intuition and the ego's narratives. Doubts regarding your connection can be healthy, as they mean you're approaching the connection with a grounded, sensible nature, and questions are intended to lead you deeper into connecting with your soul's truth versus seeking externally for answers and validation. This is all part of the ascension process. Don't be afraid of "getting it wrong," as there is no wrong—your experience, either way, has been part of your journey in loving and honoring yourself. Release the labels, which only encourage attachment, and feel the energy of the connection in your heartspace. Use the exercise, *Harmonizing the Hologram*, from Chapter Four to help you.

What's your take on False Twins or Karmic Twins?

I personally don't like the terms "false twin" or "karmic twin." If you were activated to your journey through a connection, that person carried the Twin Flame energy and served a purpose, even if they no longer continue in connection with you. This may be part of your ascension journey as a lesson in discernment.

Am I meant to come into physical sacred union?
In a word, yes. If you feel the union energy—and for some, you may have felt it your whole life without fully being conscious or understanding of it—then you're meant for physical union with a sacred partner. However, the spiritual community has highly romanticized the journey, and while romance can absolutely play a part in your human experience, it's important to release the expectations for how your physical union manifests.

Twin Flame is an energy, and there's free will on this journey where all is for the purpose of the soul's evolution. Here are a couple different scenarios I've seen playing out within the collective—be sure to only take what resonates for you and your path:

∞ You and your counterpart continue to grow together along your journey and remain (generally) energetically compatible, leading to physical union. See Chapter Seven.

∞ The counterpart who catalyzed you to your ascension journey through the sacred union path carried the Twin Flame energy for your healing phase, but they might not be meant to ascend with you as a life partner in physical union (what I like to differentiate as the Twin Soul). See Chapter One.

∞ A high-level soulmate embodying the counterpart energy enters while the Twin Flame is still undergoing their ascension or if they're in a committed relationship. (In a more-specific scenario, you might already be in a committed relationship with a soulmate.) This soulmate will be energetically compatible to reflect the growth you've experienced through your Higher-Heart Ascension as a way to keep you in the vibration of love. You might later reunite with your Twin Flame or choose the soulmate as a life partner. See Chapter Seven, *The Soulmate Path*.

How do I heal the blocks in my connection?

The blocks you're seeing in your connection are reflections of an unconscious, perpetuating belief housed within yourself that needs to be brought to the surface for acknowledgment or clearing. For example, you could be literally blocked from communicating with your counterpart, which might trigger fears of abandonment or rejection. Not only are you being asked to look at those trigger points, but where else might you be blocking yourself? Are you communicating your needs and wants in other areas of your life? Are you holding yourself back or guarding your heart in any discernable way?

The sacred union path of ascension is a deep dive into uncovering these beliefs, and Twin Flame blocks are the reflection showing you where to look. For more on healing on your journey, check out Chapters Five and Six or visit our Ascension Connections portal at www.susandawnspiritual.com.

How do I stop the runner-chaser dynamic between me and my Twin Flame?

Resistance is created when you're not in a state of surrender—when you're trying to unconsciously manipulate or control. This only keeps you disconnected from yourself and shifts you out of alignment. Look at this from a wider perspective: if you push against the Universe, the Universe pushes back. That's because you *are* the Universe pushing against itself. The same goes for your Twin Flame. If you're experiencing any kind of resistance (seen in the runner-chaser dynamic), you're simply chasing yourself. This is your own resistance. Pull that energy back to focus on yourself and anchor into trust. It's here you embrace surrender.

How do I know if I'm healed?

Your ascension journey is one of evolution, and evolution is an ever-unfolding process. Healing, too, occurs in layers and will never be complete—at least, not in the way we think it means. Your life journey itself is one of healing, which is simply another word for growth. Healing doesn't mean you're broken. It means you're deconstructing belief systems, shifting pain patterns, and transforming conditional programming. It means you're growing. What you'll experience as you continue to heal and grow is much more peace. You might experience pinpricks of residual energy, but what once triggered or hurt you won't have the same reactive effect—it might not even be part of your perceived reality anymore! The peace you feel within will be the new cornerstone from which you navigate your life. Follow the peace.

What can you tell me about Twin Flames and children?

We channeled this message a few years ago about the New Earth energy and children who are ready to incarnate or who have already incarnated through one or both Twin Flame partners. Through your healing journey, your sacred relationship positively impacts all generational lines to follow, in whichever way your connection with these souls is configured on Earth. For example, you might have children together, one Twin Flame partner might be a biological parent, or you might nurture or care for children without being a parent (as in the case of caregivers or educators). These advanced souls are here to assist in the creation of a new paradigm from higher states of consciousness. They support new parent/child dynamics that release the old, karmic authority-driven paradigm in favor of soul-to-soul connections.

Does this Twin Flame/ascension journey
ever get easier?

It does! I always say ascension isn't for the faint of heart. That's because it takes immense courage and strength to do the deep dives and inner work this journey requires. You're clearing outdated patterns and beliefs, unlocking new templates and levels of consciousness, and transforming in ways you never could have imagined. Grant yourself grace and have compassion and patience for yourself and your counterpart. As you continue your spiritual journey, a new path unwinds, and with greater curiosity and excitement, you'll step through a doorway of love with more joy, greater peace, and a lighter sense of being.

TOO LONG; DIDN'T READ
(Give me the shortened version of what this journey's about!)

You and your Twin Flame are one soul showing up in the world as two people reflecting every aspect of yourselves to clear anything from your energy that isn't love, grow into the truest expression of your authentic soul-self, and evolve in the higher consciousness frequencies of love and unity, which has ripple effects on everything around you.

Wait, let's try again…

Your sacred union is a journey of love as you, beloved and the beloved, welcome each other home in connection to the oneness of all.

One more time?

You in unity.

CHAPTER ELEVEN
FINAL THOUGHTS

"You may say I'm a dreamer, but I'm not the only one."
– John Lennon, *Imagine*

SINCE I WAS A LITTLE girl, I've always believed in love. I grew up listening to my mom's Beatles albums, crooning, "All you need is love," and devouring stories of fated encounters and love triumphing against all odds. I'm a romantic at heart, yet somehow, even my romanticism seemed to have its limits.

You have to understand, I was never the little girl who wanted to be the princess at the ball. I was more inclined to believe in a Cinderella pre-glass slipper—one who worked hard and changed her destiny versus waiting on a prince to whisk her away. Still, those stories and songs and poetry spoke to something already nestled in my heart, and I would feel the echoes of their energy as part of my soul throughout my life.

My journey of ascension has led me to claim love as I never would have dared in a previous version of myself. I've learned to welcome the softened heart and formidable strength of my Divine Feminine energy that I previously recognized in fractals but never embraced in wholeness like this. With each push from the Universe, with every energetic death and rebirth, I've gone deeper and deeper into this acceptance.

During my ascension, I didn't just look at my shadows, I journeyed to the Underworld of myself. I crawled through the trauma, dug through every fear and vulnerability, and then I did it again and again, excavating within the depths until I found more light. With that guiding light, and with the presence of supportive soul family, I continue this process even now and forever, with renewed strength and courage and faith.

It's in the throes of this journey and through the reunion of my own soul that I rediscovered the love that's always been part of my life. It was there when I was a little girl, speaking to angels on the carpet of my childhood bedroom; there in the ancient mountains of southern France, guiding my way through grief; and there in the catacombs of darkness, my saving grace through illness. It called to me in a group meditation when, in my vision, he did a little jig to make me laugh before sitting beside me in sacred silence for the whole of the session, the power of his presence overwhelming me to the point of tears. It stopped time and wove its way into my heart when I turned around one November night and locked eyes with someone I'd known my whole life but finally saw in that one moment. It sat with me in the White Spring in Glastonbury, the sacred masculine merging in homecoming with my sacred feminine, reminding me that, on this path, we never walk alone.

Anytime I felt lost, love found me. Anytime I wanted to give up, love held me. Anytime I tried to resist or deny my connection, love reminded me of its unwavering truth.

So, I surrendered, and with love came peace.

Love rarely looks like what's written about in storybooks and songs—with our attachments and conditions and limitations. We humans have a pretty bad habit of getting in our own way, and we make love so much more complicated than it needs to be. But life is messy, and that's part of its magic. In our humanness, we learn grace, compassion, and forgiveness. In our humanness, we learn sacred love.

Love is everywhere, in everything. This I've believed since I was that little girl, and it's something I've held onto my entire life. After all, my heart is nothing if not stubborn! Now I proclaim my belief in this, too…

I believe in the Sacred Masculine.

I believe in the Sacred Feminine.

I believe in Sacred Union.

This book was written through the lens of my personal journey with the intention of sharing everything I've come to understand about Twin Flames, sacred relationships, and ascension. But it's also about love.

It's also about you.

The ascension journey is a difficult one. It requires shifting perspectives, rewriting beliefs, and changing the story you've been telling or hearing about yourself for most of your life. It expects dedication to your personal growth and asks for continued patience, grace, and compassion. It demands discipline and practice to bring yourself to a new level of surrender and self-awareness time and time again, and then it challenges you to transform within that container.

On this sacred union path, when faced with your divine mirror, you're looking at your beloved as beloved. It means seeing yourself the same.

There is no other. The two are not separate.

This journey will bring you to your knees, then it will lift you back up. It will empty you out, and it will fill you to the brim. It will tear your ego down until you recognize and integrate your soul.

It is the darkest night and the brightest day, and when you start to understand the blessings that come with both—when you fear neither and embrace all—you begin to unite with the Divine within you as one always with you. You have never been forgotten. You have never been abandoned. You have never been too much or not enough, or the thousands of lies you've been fed that keep you from yourself.

This knowing goes beyond a logical, intellectual understanding. It's something that's anchored into the heart. This is what sets you free and feeds your soul. This is what creates unity. This is what brings peace.

The changes you see in your life and connection are a testament to *you*—you, who choose to embody more love every day. Choice is your free will and one of the greatest gifts given, and consciously choosing love despite the challenges of self and the facade of fear creates a ripple effect of profound significance not only in your individual life, not only in connection with another, but in the world.

You never know how far a little light can spread.

More than a decade ago, I found myself on my knees in the depths of despair and surrender. I heard God speak to me through the voice of my soul, infiltrating my guarded heart.

These words are yours now, for whenever you need them:

"Dear one, *you* are the sacred. *You* are the spiritual. *You* are the beloved. This is what you're meant to realize. As you walk this beautiful earth, you carry the codes within you. No matter where you are, no matter what you do, love always exists as part of you."

WANT MORE TWIN FLAME TEACHINGS?

Journey to Union

Accelerate your sacred union path with the Journey to Union Video Bundle!

Our remastered channelings are carefully curated and edited to help you get the most out of your journey. With over 40 videos, 16 hours of channeling, and our *Alchemy of Love* Twin Flame Workbook, this video bundle is your ultimate guide to the sacred union path of ascension.

STAY UP TO DATE!

Subscribe on YouTube for our original Sacred Union and Ascension Relationship Energy Updates, Sacred Channelings, Light Language Transmissions, and more!

Susan Dawn Spiritual Connections
&
Susan Dawn Ascension Connections

FOR YOUR JOURNEY

From healing resources to inclusive learning tools, continue your soul growth journey by exploring all of the services and products at Susan Dawn Spiritual Connections!

Ascension Connections Courses & Programs
Healing & Harmony Activation Series
Tarot in Translation Series
Meditations
Spiritual Guides & Journals
Tarot & Oracle Decks

BOOKS BY SUSAN DAWN

Daybreak: Daily Messages to Illuminate Your Spiritual Life
Get guidance when you need it most with motivational
messages that illuminate your soul growth journey! Channeled
with warmth, love, and compassion, each message in *Daybreak*
provides a prompt for conscious reflection to connect you
deeper with yourself and help you navigate your spiritual life.

ABOUT SUSAN DAWN

Susan Dawn is an author, holistic spiritual mentor, and energy practitioner at *Susan Dawn Spiritual Connections* with a focus on soul connections, conscious relationships, and the ascension journey. As a natural psychic intuitive, she serves as an intermediary to bring through guidance messages and healing activations for union with yourself, others, and the Universe by nurturing your personal empowerment and encouraging connection to your sacred creativity and authentic magic.

Connect with Susan on social media at
@susandawnspiritual!

ABOUT SUSAN DAWN SPIRITUAL CONNECTIONS

Susan Dawn Spiritual Connections is a sacred space for your soul growth journey and the home of Ascension Connections and Tarot in Translation! Bridging spiritual understanding with real, human application, *Susan Dawn Spiritual Connections* offers everything you need for your soul's expansion and to connect to your divinity within.

Learn more at www.susandawnspiritual.com

ACKNOWLEDGEMENTS

LIKE PRETTY MUCH EVERYTHING IN my life, I poured my heart and soul into this book as a labor of love for a journey that has meant so much to me. I can't express enough how deeply I appreciate everyone who has engaged in our community. You've been a beautiful part of my personal evolution, and I thank you from the bottom of my heart for the honor of being part of yours.

To Francine, who has been a spiritual mentor and friend, guiding my way as I began my journey home to myself. You're in my heart forever.

To Janet, a lover of books and a champion of writers. I didn't expect to be writing these words to you in a book such as this, but your presence has been with me through its earliest drafts and it feels all the more profound now. Thank you for reminding me that the light we shine is the legacy we leave behind. The heavens gained another star. I will miss you terribly.

To Luna & Kelly, my British soul sisters, for your love and friendship and the memory of a lifetime in the sacred gardens of Chalice Well.

To Monica, Meg, & Melissa, for being my best friends through the ages and the many stages of this wild ride. Your endless love, support, and ability to hold space is the bedrock of my journey.

To my family of soul sisters and brothers, thank you for your unconditional love and encouragement.

To the *Susan Dawn Spiritual Connections* community, thank you for your trust and acceptance as we walk each other home.

And finally, to my beloved. For *everything*.

9 798988 288138